The Deaf Child in a Hearing Family

NURTURING DEVELOPMENT

The Deaf Child in a Hearing Family

NURTURING DEVELOPMENT

Arthur Boothroyd, PhD
Janice Gatty, EdD

PLURAL
PUBLISHING
INC.

SAN DIEGO
OXFORD
BRISBANE

PLURAL PUBLISHING
INC.

5521 Ruffin Road
San Diego, CA 92123

e-mail: info@pluralpublishing.com
Web site: http://www.pluralpublishing.com

49 Bath Street
Abingdon, Oxfordshire OX14 1EA
United Kingdom

FSC
www.fsc.org
MIX
Paper from
responsible sources
FSC® C011935

Copyright © by Plural Publishing, Inc. 2012

Typeset in 11/14 Garamond by Flanagan's Publishing Services, Inc.
Printed in the United States of America by McNaughton and Gunn

Library of Congress Cataloging-in-Publication Data

Boothroyd, Arthur.
    The deaf child in the hearing family : nurturing development / Arthur Boothroyd
and Janice Gatty.
        p. ; cm.
    Includes bibliographical references and index.
    ISBN-13: 978-1-59756-394-9 (alk. paper)
    ISBN-10: 1-59756-394-3 (alk. paper)
    I. Gatty, Janice, 1950- II. Title.
    [DNLM: 1. Child. 2. Deafness--rehabilitation. 3. Child Development. 4. Hearing
Impaired Persons--psychology. 5. Infant. 6. Parent-Child Relations. WV 271]
    LC classification not assigned
    362.4'20832--dc23
                                2011031094

Contents

Preface

In 1982, Prentice Hall published Arthur Boothroyd's text *Hearing Impairments in Young Children*. Much has changed in the intervening 30 years. For example, with improvements in obstetric care, the pattern of causation among children with hearing loss has changed; genetic research has provided an abundance of detail on the causes of inherited deafness; the identification of hearing loss soon after birth has become a reality through universal newborn screening; hearing aids have shrunk in size and, through digital processing, have increased in versatility; and the multichannel cochlear implant has made it possible to provide good hearing to children with total hearing loss. Clearly, a new edition was long overdue.

Other changes have also occurred. Among them was the accumulation of experience and, perhaps wisdom, on the part of both Arthur Boothroyd and Janice Gatty. The latter was an indispensible resource during the writing of the original text and is now a coauthor. She was also the moving force behind the decision to update. When work started on the project, however, it quickly became apparent that a new edition was out of the question. What was needed was a new book.

As the title suggests, this book is still about the management of hearing loss in a child born to hearing parents who have chosen spoken language competence as one of their goals for the child. The book is addressed both to those parents and to beginning and practicing professionals in the areas of communication disorders and education of the deaf.

The book is in two parts. Part 1 provides an introduction to several disciplines that undergird the management of pediatric hearing loss. Part 2 explores the various aspects of intervention.

The authors would like to thank the teachers, staff, administration, parents, and children at the Clarke Schools for Hearing and

Speech. In particular: Jennifer Einhorn and Jessica Appleby for their help in selecting and lending us photographs taken of the children at work on the Northampton and Philadelphia campuses; Bill Corwin, the president, for his support of the project; to Judy Sexton, director of the Philadelphia campus, for assistance with the photographs; and Marian Hartblay and the staff at the Integrated Preschool and Parent-Infant programs in Northampton for listening to early drafts of narrative, but especially for continuing to provide young deaf and hearing children and their families with a rich, stimulating, and nurturing environment in which to grow and learn. In a real sense, this book belongs to them. (We wish it was as easy to relinquish responsibility for any errors.)

Although much has changed in 30 years, many things have stayed the same. Among them are the essential nature of the children and the hopes, fears, and aspirations of their parents. We dedicate this book to the many children and parents who have taught us what we know and contributed to the richness of our own lives.

PART 1

Hearing Loss and Child Development

Part 1 provides basic background information that will help both parents and professionals understand the developmental implications of hearing loss and the components of intervention. Shared knowledge of this type also facilitates communication among and between professionals and parents. In Chapter 1 we present sound and hearing as a means of perceiving events at a distance. Chapter 2 focuses on the events of human speech and the resulting sound patterns. In Chapter 3 we talk more about the sense of hearing, by which sound is detected, analyzed, and interpreted. Chapter 4 addresses the core of this work, which is child development and the role normally played in it by sound and hearing. In Chapter 5 we talk about the many things that can go wrong with hearing and in Chapter 6 we describe the ways in which hearing is assessed. Chapter 7 provides background information on hearing aids and cochlear implants. We will draw on material presented in Part 1 when we discuss intervention and management in Part 2.

Throughout each chapter in Part 1 you will find extra material in text boxes. If you are new to this material you may want to skip these boxes as first reading and return to them later. For readers who seek information beyond what is offered here we offer some suggestions for further reading.

CHAPTER 1

Hearing and Sound

Sound is what stimulates hearing, and sound is what we experience when hearing is stimulated. Use of the same word to refer both to the stimulus, and to the resulting sensation, can lead to confusion. When we need to avoid confusion, we can use the terms sound stimulus and sound sensation. These two aspects of sound have different but related properties. The sound stimulus has properties such as amplitude, frequency, and spectrum (things we can measure) whereas the sound sensation has properties such as loudness, pitch, and quality (things we experience).

Because sound travels rapidly, over considerable distances, and around corners, and because sound patterns carry information about the events that caused them, a sense of hearing is ideal for learning what is happening around us. Hearing allows us to perceive events at a distance even when they cannot be seen.

Sound patterns can be very complicated but they are made up from basic building blocks which we refer to as "pure tones." Each pure tone has only two properties, amplitude and frequency. As a result, we can illustrate any sound as a collection of points on a chart that represents frequency from left to right and amplitude from top to bottom. The audiogram form, which is used for showing the results of a basic hearing test, is ideal for this purpose. We use it in later chapters to show how hearing loss affects the ability to hear the sound patterns of speech.

Sound

Close your eyes and listen. What did you hear? A refrigerator running? A door closing? Leaves rustling? Water running? A dog barking? Someone talking? Whatever you heard, it was something happening. You didn't hear objects (things). You heard events (things happening to objects). More specifically, you heard events that involved movement of objects. One reason we can hear things happening is because we live in an ocean of air. Anything that moves disturbs the air around it. The patterns of disturbance travel away from the source in the form of invisible ripples carrying information about the event that produced them. If the patterns of disturbance have the characteristics needed to stimulate our sense of hearing, we call them "sound" and we call the invisible ripples "sound waves." A full definition of sound, therefore, is: *patterns of movement that are capable of stimulating the human sense of hearing.*

More About Sound Waves

Sound waves are similar to the ripples created on the surface of a still pond when a pebble is thrown in. But there are differences. Ripples on a pond involve up and down movements of the water, at right angles to the direction in which the ripples are traveling. Sound waves involve backward and forward movements of the air, in the direction in which sound is traveling. More importantly, these backward and forward movements produce tiny, rapid fluctuations of air pressure. The sense of hearing has evolved to detect these pressure fluctuations and convert them into patterns of nerve impulses for interpretation by the brain.

We can also define sound as: *the sensation evoked when the sense of hearing is stimulated.* If we need to avoid confusion we can use the terms *sound stimulus* and *sound sensation.* There can be a sound stimulus without a sound sensation (think of a totally deaf person). And there can be a sound sensation without a sound stimulus (think of tinnitus—also known as ringing in the ears).

More About the Word Sound

If a tree falls in the forest and nobody is there to hear it, does it make a sound?

This is not a philosophical puzzle but illustrates a problem caused by using the same word to refer to two different things. The falling tree makes a sound stimulus but, if nobody is there to hear it, there is no sound sensation.

Hearing

Hearing is the sense that detects and interprets sound. It allows us to monitor and recognize events in our environment even when we can't see the objects involved, as illustrated in Figure 1–1. Although

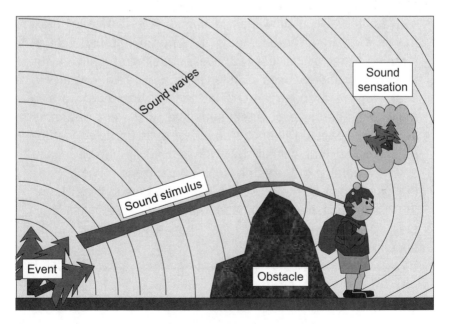

Figure 1–1. Sound and hearing make possible the timely perception of events at a distance, even when they cannot be seen.

it is events that we hear, we can often identify the objects involved. If you hear a car starting, for example, you may say, "I heard a car." But this is possible only if you have learned to associate the object with the event, and both with the resulting sound. Sometimes your inference will be wrong. One of us recalls, as a child, being puzzled by the sound of speech coming from the radio and concluding that there must be tiny people living inside the cabinet (and wondering who fed them).

More About Sound and Hearing

Hearing takes advantage of three important properties of sound. First, it travels through the air, freeing us of the need to touch things in order to figure out what is going on. Second, it travels rapidly, covering around 1100 feet, or 300 meters, in a second. As a result, we can detect and recognize events almost as soon as they occur. Third, sound travels around corners by a process called diffraction. This feature enables us to detect and recognize events that we can't see.

But there is a drawback to sound. It gets weaker as it travels away from the source. In the open air, around 75% of a sound's strength is lost with every doubling of distance. By the time sound reaches a listener, it can be very weak. To deal with this problem, nature has found a variety of ways to make our hearing exquisitely sensitive. If it were any more sensitive, we would hear the sound of dust particles jostling around in our ear canals. But with sensitivity comes vulnerability. According to the World Health Organization (WHO), hearing loss is one of the most common of all disabilities. Using 2005 statistics, it was estimated that around 278 million people had significant hearing loss. That is, 4% of the world's population.

The Pure Tone

The value of sound is not just its presence but the information contained in its patterns. The simplest sound pattern is that of the pure tone. In a pure tone, the fluctuations of air pressure are smooth, regular, and repetitive. A pure tone has only two properties: frequency, which is the rate at which the pattern of pressure fluctuation repeats itself, and amplitude, which is the size of the fluctuations. We express frequency in hertz (Hz) and amplitude in decibels (dB).

More About Frequency and Amplitude

Frequency is *the rate at which the basic pattern of pressure fluctuation repeats itself.* It is expressed in cycles per second. One cycle per second is also referred to as one hertz, abbreviated to Hz. This term is used to honor a German scientist credited with the discovery of radio waves. Pure tones with frequencies in the range of 20 Hz to 20,000 Hz are capable of stimulating the human sense of hearing and, therefore, meet the definition of sound given earlier. Changes of frequency in a sound stimulus are heard as changes of pitch in the resulting sound sensation.

Amplitude is *the size of the pressure fluctuations in the sound wave.* We prefer not to express amplitude directly in terms of pressure but in terms of the energy carried by the sound. For this purpose we used decibels, or dB. This term is used to honor Alexander Graham Bell who is credited with the invention of the telephone. The number in dB tells us how many times stronger a sound is than some reference sound. The strength of the reference sound is either stated or implied. For more information, see Table 1–1.

Table 1–1. Converting "How Many Times Stronger" to deciBels (for the mathematically inclined)

How many times stronger than the reference sound	Count the number of zeros after the "1" to get the number of Bels	Then multiply by ten to convert to deciBels	
10,000,000,000	10	100	
1,000,000,000	9	90	
100,000,000	8	80	
10,000,000	7	70	
1,000,000	6	60	
100,000	5	50	
10,000	4	40	
1,000	3	30	
100	2	20	
10	1	10	
1	0	0	← Reference sound
0.1	−1	−10	
0.01	−2	−20	

For numbers that are not multiples of 10		
2 times	=	3 dB
3 times	=	5 dB
4 times	=	6 dB
5 times	=	7 dB
6 or 7 times	=	8 dB
8 times	=	9 dB
9 or 10 times	=	10 dB

Notes:

1. The reference sound automatically has a value of 0 dB (there were no zeros after the 1).
2. 0 dB does not mean "no sound." It is simply the level of the reference sound.
3. Each 10 dB step represents a 10-fold increase in sound strength.
4. There can be negative dB values.
5. To combine two multipliers we add the dB.
   For example: 3000 times = 3 × 1000 times = 5 dB + 30 dB = 35 dB
6. If *really* want to know: Level in dB = $10*\log_{10}(H)$ where H is, "How many times stronger."

A single pure tone doesn't carry much information, but pure tones are the building blocks of all sounds. Just as simple stone blocks (of various shapes and sizes) can be combined and arranged to create a cathedral, so simple pure tones (of various frequencies and amplitudes) can be combined and arranged to create a symphony. For this reason, pure tones are one of the tools used to test hearing. By finding the amplitude of the weakest pure tone a child can hear at each of several frequencies we learn something about the sensitivity of her hearing and about her potential for getting information from more complex sounds such as the sounds of speech. The results of a pure-tone hearing test constitute an *audiogram* and are usually recorded on an *audiogram form* as symbols, joined by a line. We discuss audiograms in Chapter 5.

The Audiogram Form

The audiogram form is simply a chart showing frequency from left to right and amplitude from top to bottom. Although this form is designed for recording the results of hearing tests, it also has other uses. In Figure 1–2, we use it to illustrate the frequency and amplitude range of human hearing and the relationship of frequency and amplitude, which are properties of the sound stimulus, to pitch and loudness, which are the corresponding properties of the sound sensation. Low-frequency (low-pitched) sounds are on the left and high-frequency (high-pitched) sounds are on the right. For historical reasons, the amplitude scale is upside down. Weak (quiet) sounds are at the top and strong (loud) sounds are at the bottom. The horizontal line labeled 0 dB HL represents the weakest pure tone at each frequency that is just detectable to a typical young adult with normal hearing. The shaded area above this line contains tones that are too weak to be heard. The shaded area at the bottom of the chart contains tones that are too loud for comfort—and potentially damaging. The full frequency range of human hearing is from 20 to 20,000 Hz but hearing tests are usually limited to the range from 125 to 8000 Hz, and so is the audiogram form. This frequency range contains most of the useful information in sound patterns. The heavy line in Figure 1–2 encloses the *area of normal hearing* within which pure tones are audible, tolerable, and useful.

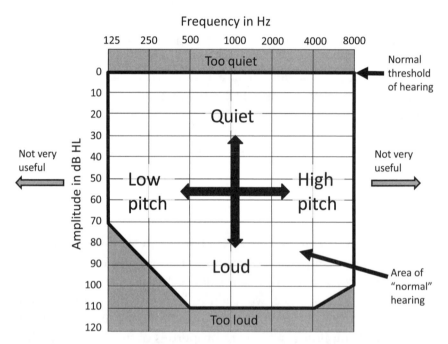

Figure 1–2. The audiogram form is used, here, to illustrate the relationship between two properties of a sound stimulus (frequency and amplitude) and the corresponding properties of the resulting sound sensation (pitch and loudness). It also defines an "area" of normal hearing in which sounds are audible, tolerable, and useful.

More About the Audiogram Form

1. Note that *equal steps* on the frequency scale represent *equal multiplications of frequency*. Because of the way the hearing mechanism works, however, they are heard as equal changes of pitch.

2. In contrast, *equal steps* on the amplitude scale represent *equal additions of decibels*. In reality, however, each increase of 10 decibels represents a 10-fold multiplication of sound strength. Just as the hearing system hears equal multiplications of frequency as equal steps of pitch, so it hears equal multiplications of strength as equal steps of loudness. The decibel scale already takes account of this fact.

3. The 110 dB amplitude range of normal hearing means that we can tolerate sounds that are 100,000,000,000 times as strong as the weakest sounds we can detect. We hope you are as impressed with this fact as we are. Note, however, that prolonged and repeated exposure to sounds in excess of 80 dB HL can damage hearing.

The Sound Spectrum

Isolated pure tones seldom occur in nature. The closest you come to generating a pure tone is when you whistle. Most sounds are combinations of many pure tones, each with its own frequency and amplitude. A sound's *spectrum* is *a listing of the frequencies and amplitudes of its constituent pure tones*. This listing can be represented as a table but is more commonly shown as a graph. The spectrum of a sound stimulus contributes to the quality of the resulting sound sensation. It is an important source of evidence about the event that caused the sound. Complex sounds can be placed into two major groups: complex tones and random noise.

1. In complex tones, the sound stimulus has a spectrum consisting of discrete pure tones whose frequencies are related to each other in an orderly manner. The resulting sound sensation has a definite pitch, which is usually determined by the tone with the lowest frequency, otherwise known as the *fundamental frequency.* The quality of the sound sensation depends on the way amplitude varies with frequency. Examples of complex tones include the sounds of most musical instruments and, in speech, the vowels such as "oo," "ah," and "ee." The top panel of Figure 1–3 illustrates the spectrum of a complex tone on an audiogram form. Each dot represents one of the pure tones making up this sound pattern.

2. Random noise has a less organized spectrum with many pure tones whose frequencies have no orderly relationship to each other. The resulting sensation has no definite pitch, but the quality still depends on the way amplitude varies with frequency. Examples include the sound of rushing water and, in speech, the consonants "s" and "sh." The middle panel of Figure 1–3 illustrates the spectrum of a random noise. In this case, the dots are so closely spaced that they create a line.

Speech, as a sound stimulus, is a mixture of complex tones and random noises whose amplitudes and spectra vary rapidly from moment to moment. We can illustrate the time variation using an area—as shown in the bottom panel of Figure 1–3. In this case, we are showing the range of frequencies and amplitudes of the constituent tones in the speech of a typical talker, heard at a conversational level. Because of its appearance, this area is often referred to as the "speech banana."

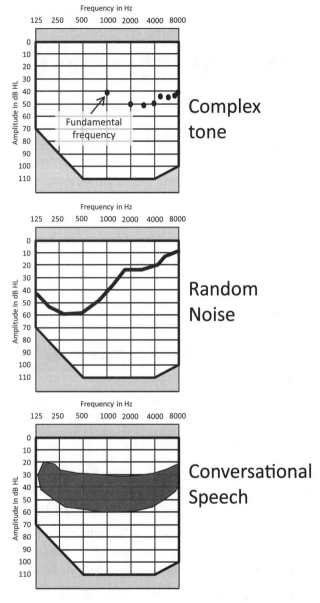

Figure 1–3. The audiogram form is used here to illustrate sound spectra. The top panel shows a complex tone with a fundamental frequency of 1000 Hz. Each dot is a pure tone. The middle panel shows a random noise. The bottom panel shows the frequency and amplitude range covered by the sounds of typical conversational speech.

Physical and Psychological Dimensions of Sound

The sound stimulus has physical dimensions of frequency, fundamental frequency, amplitude, spectrum, and time variation. With suitable instruments, these properties can be measured and expressed in numbers. The sound sensation has psychological dimensions such as pitch, loudness, and quality. These properties can be measured only by asking people to report what they hear. The properties of a sound sensation depend on the properties of the sound stimulus. Loudness depends mainly on amplitude; pitch depends mainly on frequency (for pure tones) or fundamental frequency (for complex tones); and quality depends on both spectrum and patterns of change over time.

Some Things to Remember

1. A **sound stimulus** consists of *vibrations that are capable of stimulating the human sense of hearing.*

2. A **sound sensation** is *the sensation experienced when the sense of hearing is stimulated.*

3. **Hearing** enables us to detect and identify events at a distance, almost as soon as they occur, even if they cannot be seen.

4. The simplest sound stimulus is the **pure tone**. It has only two properties: frequency (rate of vibration, measured in Hz) and amplitude (size of vibration, measured in dB).

5. **Complex sounds** are combinations of many pure tones.

6. The **spectrum** of a complex sound is a listing (or picture) of the frequencies of its constituent pure tones together with the amplitude of each one.

7. The **audiogram form** can be used to show the spectrum of a sound stimulus. For complicated sounds like speech, which vary over time, we show an area.

8. The properties of a **sound stimulus** determine the properties of the resulting *sound sensation.*

   ■ Differences of **frequency** (or fundamental frequency) are heard as differences of *pitch.*

   ■ Differences of **amplitude** are heard as differences of *loudness.*

   ■ Differences of **spectrum** and *patterns of change over time* are heard as differences of *sound quality.*

Relevance

Our goal is to minimize the impact of childhood hearing loss on development in general and the development of spoken language in particular. Speech sounds are produced by rapid, coordinated, complex movements of various parts of the speech mechanism, most of which cannot be seen. The sound patterns of speech provide evidence about the speech movements (events) that caused them and about the language patterns (words and sentences) they represent. These language patterns provide evidence about meaning. Hearing loss limits a child's access to the information carried by the sounds of speech, including his own. We will be calling on material covered in this chapter as we explore the mechanisms of hearing, the nature of hearing loss, the properties of spoken language, the developmental impact of hearing loss, the technology used to provide a child with access to the information carried by sound and, when we deal with management in Part 2, ways to enrich the child's environment and experiences to promote the development of hearing skills.

To Learn More

■ Sound and its behavior are complex topics. There are courses, degrees, professions, texts, and journals devoted exclusively to these topics. They fall under such headings as "Acoustics," "Underwater Acoustics," "Acoustical Engineering," and "Architectural Acoustics." Unfortunately, it is difficult to delve further into this topic without encountering mathematics; some of it quite daunting.

■ For those readers who are not deterred by math, we suggest Speaks's 1999 text *Introduction to Sound: Acoustics for the Hearing and Speech Sciences.*

■ If you want to avoid the math, we recommend Chapter 2 of *The Acoustics of Speech Communication* by Pickett, also published in 1999.

■ More information on hearing is provided in Chapter 3 of the present text.

CHAPTER 2

The Sounds of Speech

Overview

In Chapter 1, we showed that hearing and sound make possible the perception of events at a distance. In this chapter, we deal with the specific events involved in speech. Speech is produced by finely controlled movements of systems originally evolved for breathing, eating, and drinking. In English, we use only three methods of creating sound. As the resulting sounds pass through the mouth and/or nose, however, their spectra are shaped to create a wide variety of sound patterns. These patterns of speech movement and sound are grouped into phoneme classes, based on their ability to affect word meaning. Spoken words and sentences are created by combining, in sequence, sounds from one or more phoneme classes. Additional patterns, such as rhythm and melody are then created. The pure-tone building blocks of the sound patterns of speech cover a wide range of frequencies but the most useful region is from around 1000 to around 3500 Hz. Basic knowledge of the sound patterns of speech, and the distribution of useful information in these patterns, is key to understanding the impact of hearing impairment and hearing assistance on a child's ability to develop and use spoken language.

The Speech Mechanism

The sounds of speech are produced by coordinated actions of muscles controlling the lungs, the vocal folds, the tongue, the jaw, the lips, and the velum (the flap at the back of the palate that can be raised to stop liquids, air, and sound from passing through the nose). The various parts of this mechanism originally evolved for eating, drinking, swallowing, and breathing. In humans, they have been co-opted and adapted for speech production. Figure 2–1 provides a simplified view of this mechanism in cross-section.

Control and coordination of the various parts of the speech mechanism are the responsibility of the brain. To be effective, the brain needs information about both the target sound patterns and the success of efforts to match them (feedback). In the developing child, these two pieces of information are provided by the sense of hearing. The child hears the speech of people in her environment and also hears her own speech efforts. A totally deaf child trying

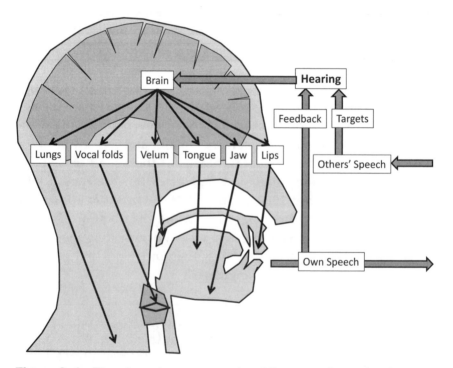

Figure 2–1. The six main components of the speech mechanism are controlled and coordinated by the brain. Hearing plays an essential role in development by providing the brain with information about the sound targets and feedback about the child's success in matching them.

to talk is rather like a blind archer who cannot see the target and doesn't know where his arrow has gone. Hearing is essential for the spontaneous development of natural-sounding speech. The brain and hearing, therefore, are included in Figure 2–1 as components of the speech mechanism.

More About Speech Control

Hearing is key to the development of speech skills. As these skills are mastered, however, hearing begins to lose its importance for speech production. By puberty, speech articulation is largely controlled by motor memory, touch, and proprioception (awareness of the positions and movements of various parts of the body). Hearing remains important, however, for control of loudness, pitch, and voice quality. An adult who suddenly loses hearing will have trouble with these three properties but still will be able to produce speech that is intelligible to others.

Making Speech Sounds

There are several ways of making sound with the speech mechanism. In English, we use only three: voicing, frication, and stop-plosion.

1. **Voicing** is produced by gently bringing the vocal folds together and passing air between them. This causes the folds to vibrate and the air to be released in a rapid series of bursts. The result is a complex tone (as in the top panel of Figure 1–3). The fundamental frequency of voicing can be varied by changing the air pressure in the lungs, the tension in the vocal folds, or both. In the typical man, the average fundamental frequency is around 100 Hz. While speaking, however, the frequency can range from around 70 to around 200 Hz to create melody, or intonation, in sentences. In women, these values are almost doubled and in children they are higher still.

2. **Frication** is produced by forcing air through a small gap. This process creates turbulent airflow—just like white water in a narrow, fast-flowing river. The result is a random noise (as in the middle panel of Figure 1–3). Speech sounds produced in this way are referred to as fricatives (e.g., "s" and "sh").

3. **Stop-plosion** involves the temporary interruption of airflow followed by release of the pressure that has built up. During the release, there is turbulent flow producing random noise but it is very short-lived. We typically refer to sounds produced in this way as stops (e.g., "p" and "t").

Voicing is always produced in the larynx but frication and stop-plosion can be produced at several places in the mouth. These methods of producing sound are used either alone or in combination. In English, voicing is the sole source for the vowels, the nasal consonants (e.g., "m" and "n"), and some vowel-like consonants (e.g., "r" and "l"). By adding voicing to frication, we get voiced fricatives (e.g., "v" and "z"). Adding voicing to stop-plosion produces voiced-stops (e.g., "b" and "d"). We have one sound that adds frication to stop-plosion (the affricate "ch"), and one that uses all three methods (the voiced affricate "dge"). There are languages that use other ways of making sound (e.g., whistles and clicks) but in English we are satisfied with these three.

Shaping Speech Sounds

Before it can be heard by a listener, any sound produced within the speech mechanism must pass through the mouth, the nose, or both. On the way, the sound's spectrum is shaped by the acoustic characteristics of these cavities. Basically, the cavities act like filters, suppressing certain frequencies in the spectrum of the original sound and allowing others through. As a result, the spectrum of the emerging sound has frequency regions of maximum energy, or formants, as illustrated in Figure 2–2. Formant frequencies are determined by the shapes and sizes of the cavities that created them.

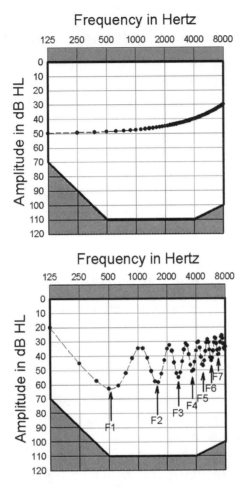

Figure 2–2. The upper panel shows the spectrum of voicing as produced by the vocal folds vibrating at a frequency of 125 Hz. The lower panel shows the spectrum of the same sound after passing through the mouth. The formants (regions of maximum energy) are numbered in sequence, starting with the lowest frequency. (Remember that amplitude increases as one goes down on this chart.) These spectra were not made from actual speech but are idealized for purposes of illustration.

In Chapter 1, we said that hearing tells us about events at a distance. When we hear speech, we learn both about the events involved in the production of sound and about the events involved in shaping the sound spectrum.

More About Shaping Speech Sounds

Several "articulators" help shape the spectrum of speech sounds. The velum can be lowered or raised (to connect or disconnect the oral and nasal cavities); the tongue can be raised or lowered and moved forward or backward in the mouth; the jaw can be raised or lowered; and the lips can be rounded or spread, pulled back or pushed out. Combinations of these features with the three kinds of sound source provide a virtually unlimited range of possibilities for making sound patterns from which each language uses a limited selection.

More About Formants

Formants are frequency regions of maximum energy in the spectrum of a speech sound. They are produced in the cavities of the nose and mouth by a process called resonance, that is, the easy transmission of those pure tones in the original sound whose frequencies correspond with the cavity's natural frequencies of vibration. The mouth cavity has many natural frequencies of vibration. We number the resulting formants in order, starting with the lowest frequency, as shown in Figure 2–2. The frequency of the first formant (F1) depends mainly on the height of the tongue and jaw. In a man it averages around 500 Hz but can vary between around 300 and 1000 Hz as the tongue and jaw are raised and lowered. The frequency of the second formant (F2) depends mainly on the size and shape of the cavity in front of the tongue. In a man, it averages around 1500 Hz but can vary between around 900 and 3000 Hz as the tongue is moved backward and forward (and the lips are rounded or spread). The second formant carries a major portion of the information in speech. The average values of higher formants increase in steps of around 1000 Hz. Their frequencies do not vary as much as those of the first two. Because women have smaller mouth cavities, the average frequencies of their formants are about 15% higher than those of men. Children's formant frequencies are higher still.

Information and the Speech Spectrum

In Figure 1–3, we showed the area covered by the sounds of speech but useful information is not spread uniformly over this area. The most important region is between 1000 and 3500 Hz. This is the region covered by the second vocal-tract formant. The frequency of this formant depends mainly on the size of the cavity in front of the tongue. If a child can hear the second formant, and follow its frequency changes over time, he learns a lot about what is happening to the talker's tongue.

Figure 2–3 covers the speech banana with open dots. The more dots there are in a given area, the more important that area is. There are 100 dots altogether. So counting the dots in a given region gives an impression of the percentage of the speech information contained in that region. You will see that roughly 60% of the dots fall between 1000 and 3500 Hz.

More About Counting Dots

The technique of counting dots was first introduced by Mueller and Killion in 1990. It offers a simple, visually based, way to estimate the percentage of the speech information that is present in different frequency regions. It is particularly useful when the speech banana is combined with the results of a pure-tone hearing test. One can then estimate the percentage of speech information available to an individual listener. We will use the count-the-dots technique later when discussing hearing loss and sensory management.

Frequency in Hz

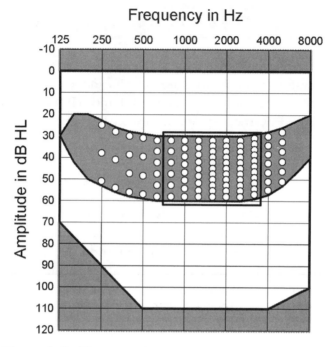

Figure 2–3. The speech banana shows the frequency and amplitude range covered by the sounds of *conversational* speech. In this figure, we add 100 dots whose distribution illustrates the relative importance of different frequency regions. Roughly 60% of the dots lie between 1000 and 3500 Hz, and between 30 and 60 dB. This is the region covered by the second vocal-tract formant. The frequency of this formant is determined by the shape and size of the cavity in front of the tongue. The dots in this figure are left open to distinguish them from the filled dots of Figure 2–2 which represent actual pure tones.

Phonemes and the Speech Banana

Another popular way of enhancing the speech banana is to show the regions that are key to identifying specific speech sounds.

Although this approach is far from precise, it does give a good impression of the contribution of different frequency regions to the sound system of spoken English. You will see from Figure 2–4 that the recognition of vowels, vowel-like consonants, and nasals depends mainly on the lower frequencies (below 2000 Hz) whereas the recognition of fricative consonants and stops depends mainly on the higher frequencies (above 2000 Hz).

More About Phonemes

Each language uses a limited set of movement and sound patterns for generating speech. At the level of short segments, these patterns are grouped into classes we call *phonemes*. A phoneme is not a specific sound but a class of sounds whose members can all serve the same purpose in defining word meaning. When we combine several sounds to make a word, the exact details of each sound don't matter so long as it comes from the right class. But if we use a sound from a different class we change the meaning of the word. The same thing happens in writing. "Sit," "SIT," "sit," and "*sit*" all mean the same thing. But "Sip" means something different.

In speech, the exact movements and positions used to produce an example of a given phoneme vary according to the sounds that come before and after (a process called co-articulation), they also vary over multiple productions of the same word by a given talker, and they can vary dramatically from talker to talker. So, too, do the resulting sound patterns, which is one reason that pictures like Figure 2–4 should not be over-interpreted. The developing child has to learn the key features that identify a specific phoneme while ignoring the many sources of variation.

For future reference, a phoneme may be defined as *a class of speech sound patterns whose members can be substituted for each other without changing perceived word meaning*.

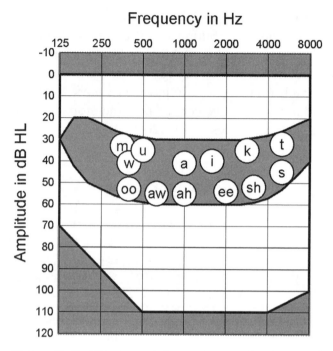

Figure 2–4. The speech banana can also be used to show the regions of most importance for the recognition of a sample of speech sounds. We have used conventional spelling here rather than phonetic symbols.

Suprasegmentals

In Figure 2–1, we showed the regions of most importance for the recognition of a sample of speech sounds — or speech segments. But speech is much more than a string of sounds. It has pitch, melody, rate, and rhythm. Melody is determined by the way pitch varies over time. Rate and rhythm are determined by the durations and relative durations of sounds, syllables, and words plus the variations of amplitude over time. Because they involve many segments, or phonemes, these aspects of the acoustic speech signal are referred to as suprasegmentals. In theory, they can be perceived from any region of the speech banana but they are best perceived in the region from around 300 Hz to around 1000 Hz (which is the region covered by the first vocal-tract formant). Contrary to popular belief, one does not need to hear the fundamental frequency itself in order to perceive the pitch and melody of speech. This information can be obtained from higher frequencies.

Some Things to Remember

1. **Speech** is produced by movement of several systems that were originally evolved for eating, drinking, swallowing, and breathing. These systems are controlled and coordinated by the brain.

2. **Hearing** plays a key role as the brain learns how to produce speech. It does so by providing the brain with models from other talkers and feedback from the learner's own efforts. For the developing child, hearing is essential for the development of natural-sounding speech.

3. Each spoken language uses a **limited set** of movement and sound patterns as building blocks for creating meaningful words.

4. These patterns can be grouped into **phoneme classes**, determined by their ability to influence word meaning (two sounds belong to different phoneme classes if substituting one for the other can change word meaning).

5. The events of speech include both movements that actually generate sound (in English, voicing, frication, and stop-plosion), and movements that **shape the spectrum** of that sound. The latter movements are of the velum, jaw, lips, and tongue, the last being the most important.

6. **Spectral shaping** produces several regions of maximum energy in the emerging sounds. We refer to these regions as

formant*s* and number them in sequence, starting with the one with the lowest frequency.

7. The **second formant** is the most informative to the listener because it provides information about tongue position and movement.

8. The spectral distribution of speech on an audiogram form (the speech banana) can be rendered more useful by adding dots to show the distribution of **useful information**. Sixty percent of this information lies between 1000 and 3500 Hz, which is the region covered by the second formant.

9. The *speech banana* can also be rendered more useful by showing the regions containing most of the information contributing to recognition of specific **phonemes**.

Relevance

We want the child both to hear speech and to learn how to produce speech. A basic understanding of speech as a motor activity, an acoustic signal, and a phoneme system can help clinicians and teachers understand the impact of hearing loss and the role of sensory management. It can also help them diagnose difficulties and plan activities to optimize hearing capacity, hearing skill, and cognitive-linguistic development. To put it simply, the more you understand about speech, the better your chances of helping the child reach her full potential in this department.

To Learn More

■ A very thorough presentation of speech acoustics and production is available in Part 1 of Pickett's 1999 text on the acoustics of speech communication.

■ You can also find more information in Chapter 17, by Boothroyd, in Madel and Flexer's 2008 text on pediatric audiology.

■ The Articulation Index (AI) was first introduced in 1949 by French and Steinberg in their paper on factors governing the intelligibility of speech sounds.

■ Their methods were subsequently standardized by the American National Standards Institute (ANSI), and published as standard S3.5-1969, "Methods for Calculating Articulation Index."

■ The process was updated with ANSI standard S3.5-1997 and the metric was renamed Speech Intelligibility Index (SII).

■ A useful Web site for calculating these two quantities for a person with hearing loss, listening to conversational speech, is available at http://www.audiologyinfo.com/cgi-bin/ai.cgi .

■ For more information on the counting-dots approach to estimating Articulation Index, see Mueller and Killion (1990).

CHAPTER 3

Hearing Mechanisms and Hearing Processes

Overview

Hearing is the sense that responds to sound. In this chapter, we explore this sense in more detail. It has three main parts, each with its own contribution to the hearing process. The conductive mechanism, consisting of the outer and middle ears, collects the sound stimulus and delivers it to the sensorineural mechanism. The sensorineural mechanism translates patterns of sound into patterns of chemical and electrical stimulation in the auditory nerve. The auditory nerve delivers these patterns of stimulation to the central mechanism, which is the brain, where they create sound sensations. The brain analyzes, integrates, and interprets the sensations and makes decisions about the nature and location of the events that produced the sound. Impairments can occur in any one of these three mechanisms.

Hearing Mechanisms

In Chapter 1, we described hearing as a sense for perceiving events at a distance from the sounds they produce. This sense uses three mechanisms, as illustrated in Figure 3–1. The first is the conductive mechanism, which *collects* sound and *delivers* it to the

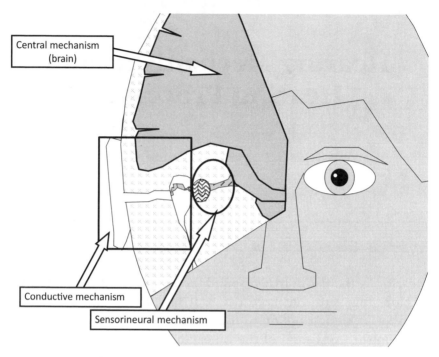

Central mechanism
(brain)

Conductive mechanism

Sensorineural mechanism

Figure 3–1. Three hearing mechanisms.

second mechanism. This is the sensorineural mechanism, where patterns of sound (acoustic evidence) are *translated* into patterns of nerve impulses (sensory evidence). These patterns are delivered to the third mechanism, the central mechanism, otherwise known as the brain.

It is in the brain that decisions are made about the presence of sound, the qualities of the sound sensation, the event that produced it, and the meaning and implications of that event. If you think of the hearing mechanism as a team given the task of interpreting sound, the conductive mechanism houses the deliverers, the sensorineural mechanism houses the translators, and the central mechanism houses the analysts, decision-makers, and responders. Figure 3–2 illustrates this analogy.

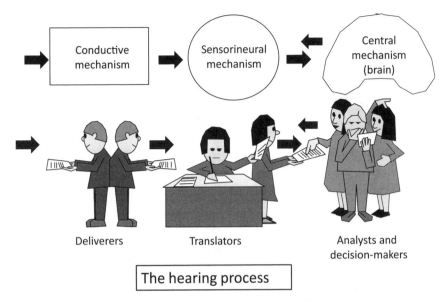

Figure 3–2. A conceptual model of hearing.

Conductive Mechanism

The conductive mechanism (Figure 3–3) includes the outer ear, which collects sound, and the ear canal, which delivers it to the eardrum membrane (technically known as the tympanic membrane, and usually referred to just as the eardrum). The eardrum vibrates in response to the tiny fluctuations of air pressure, replicating the original movements that caused the sound. On the other side of the eardrum is the middle ear. This is an air-filled cavity, bridged by a chain of three tiny bones (the ossicles), which carry movement patterns from the eardrum to the oval window membrane and on to the fluids of the sensorineural mechanism. A tube (the eustachian tube) connects the middle ear cavity to the throat. This tube is normally closed but opens from time to time to let air in or out. The purpose is to keep the same pressure on both sides of the eardrum membrane so that it can vibrate freely.

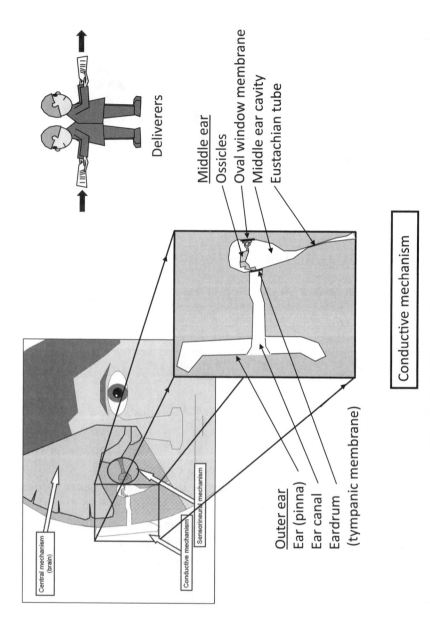

Deliverers

Middle ear
Ossicles
Oval window membrane
Middle ear cavity
Eustachian tube

Outer ear
Ear (pinna)
Ear canal
Eardrum
(tympanic membrane)

Central mechanism
(brain)

Conductive mechanism

Sensorineural mechanism

Conductive mechanism

Figure 3–3. The conductive mechanism.

Comparing Hearing and Vision

Both hearing and vision allow us to perceive objects and events at a distance. But:

1. Vision is mainly about perceiving objects. We can perceive events with vision, but only when we can see the objects involved.

2. Hearing is mainly about perceiving events. We can perceive objects with hearing, but only when we can hear the events involved.

3. Vision requires a direct line of sight. If something is happening around a corner, we may hear it but we cannot see it.

4. We can close our eyes but we cannot close our ears. Even when we sleep, our hearing is still at work. In a very real sense, hearing is our "watchdog" sense.

5. Vision provides very good detail about patterns in space but poor detail about patterns in time. In contrast, hearing provides very good detail about patterns in time (i.e., sound) but not about patterns in space. You can recognize a friend by seeing her face or by hearing her voice. But you cannot hear her face and you cannot see her voice.

6. Nevertheless, some parts of the speech mechanism are visible. In face-to-face communication, the senses of hearing and vision can both contribute to perception of the movement patterns of speech and, therefore, of the underlying language patterns. Hearing and lipreading complement and support each other.

More About the Conductive Mechanism

1. The ear canal protects the eardrum from injury and provides it with the warm humid environment needed for maximum flexibility.

2. The shape and size of the head, the ear, and the ear canal help to enhance those parts of the speech spectrum, between 1000 and 3500 Hz, which carry most of the useful information in the acoustic speech signal (see Chapter 2). In other words, this part of the conductive mechanism modifies sound patterns to emphasize the most useful features of speech.

3. The ossicular chain does more than just deliver movement patterns across the middle ear cavity. On the other side of the oval window membrane there is fluid—essentially water. Sound travels well in air and it travels well in water. But it does not travel easily from one to the other. The shapes and configuration of the tympanic membrane and the ossicles are such as to improve energy transfer from air to water about a thousand-fold, representing a 30 dB improvement in sensitivity (see Table 1–1).

Sensorineural Mechanism

The sensorineural mechanism includes the cochlea and the auditory nerve, as shown in Figure 3–4. The cochlea is a fluid-filled tube containing membranes and specialized cells. It is coiled like a snail shell into a volume not much bigger than an aspirin tablet.

If we could unroll the cochlea, as depicted in Figure 3–5, it would be around one inch (2.5 cm) long. The cochlea is divided along its length by the cochlear partition. This partition is bounded at the bottom by the basilar membrane and at the top by Reissner's membrane.

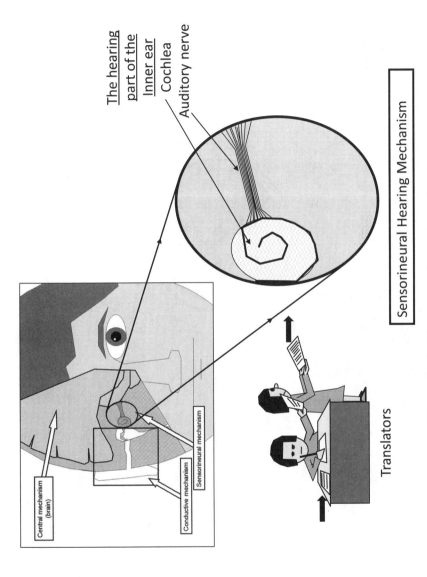

The hearing part of the
Inner ear
Cochlea
Auditory nerve

Central mechanism (brain)

Conductive mechanism

Sensorineural mechanism

Sensorineural Hearing Mechanism

Translators

Figure 3–4. The sensorineural mechanism.

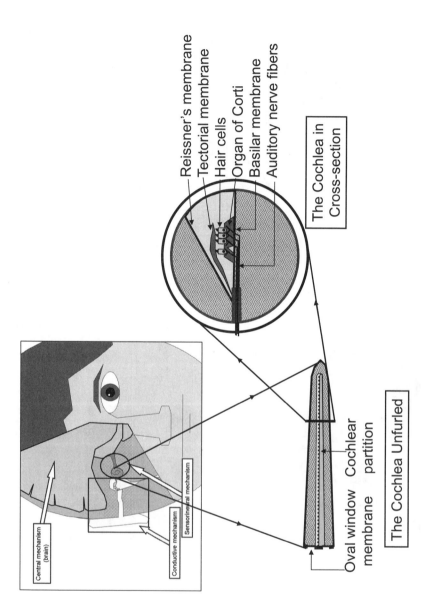

Reissner's membrane
Tectorial membrane
Hair cells
Organ of Corti
Basilar membrane
Auditory nerve fibers

The Cochlea in Cross-section

Central mechanism (brain)

Sensorineural mechanism

Conductive mechanism

Oval window   Cochlear
membrane   partition

The Cochlea Unfurled

Figure 3–5. Details of the structure of the cochlea.

Sitting on the basilar membrane is the organ of Corti which supports between 12,000 and 16,000 tiny hair cells arranged in four rows (also shown in Figure 3–5). Each cell carries a bundle of tiny projections called cilia. A third membrane, the tectorial membrane, lies over the hair cells. The hair cells are so named because the cilia look like little hairs. But they have nothing in common with the hairs on your head.

Vibrations of the ossicular chain are transferred to the oval window membrane where they produce up-and-down disturbances of the cochlear partition. These disturbances travel along the partition in the form of ripples (traveling waves). As the partition moves up and down, the cilia bend, causing electrical and chemical changes in the hair cells. These changes are transmitted to nerve fibers that make connections (synapses) with the hair cells. The resulting patterns of nerve impulses are carried by the auditory nerve to auditory centers in the brain for analysis and decision making. The auditory nerve is a bundle of around 30,000 nerve fibers. Most of these fibers carry nerve impulses to the brain and are activated by the inner row of hair cells. Some, however, carry nerve impulses in the other direction. They mainly connect with the three outer rows of hair cells, which function like tiny muscles to keep the cochlea functioning as efficiently as possible. The outer hair cells play a key role in giving us our exquisite sensitivity to sound. The fact that messages come back to the cochlea from higher brain centers is illustrated by the reverse arrow in Figure 3–2. The decision-makers are providing feedback to the translators.

Central Mechanism

The central hearing mechanism consists of auditory centers in the brainstem, the auditory portion of the brain's cortex, and all other centers in the brain that are involved in perceptual decision-making. At each level, information is extracted from the patterns of nerve stimulation. Some of this information is passed on to higher centers for further examination. Some is passed back to lower

More About the Cochlea

The cochlea's task is not just to generate nerve impulses. It also separates complex sounds into their constituent pure tones—just as a prism separates white light into its constituent colors. When waves travel along the cochlear partition, high-frequency components of the sound spectrum produce their maximum effect close to the oval window whereas lower frequency components produce their maximum effect farther along. As a result, the patterns of nerve impulses delivered to the brain (the sensory evidence) are defined not only by the way they are distributed in *time* but also by the *place* along the cochlear partition from which they came.

As the cochlea translates patterns of movement into patterns of nerve activation, it has the responsibility to preserve detail. In other words, significant changes in the sound stimulus should produce detectable changes in the sound sensation. When listening to pure tones, persons with normal hearing can distinguish over 100 different amplitude levels between 0 and 110 dB HL, and over 1000 different frequencies between 125 and 8000 Hz. They can also detect time differences between the two ears of the order of 10 millionths of a second. This impressive performance is seriously compromised when there is damage to the sensorineural mechanism.

centers, even to the cochlea, to help maintain optimal sensitivity and resolution.

Those parts of the brain responsible for interpreting the sensory evidence may make decisions about such things as:

a. Was there a sound?

b. What was it like?

c. Where did it come from?

d. What event produced it?

e. What objects were involved?

f. What are the implications of this event?

If the answer to, "What event produced it" is, "Someone talking," the decisions may involve such things as:

a. What were the gender, age, health, nationality, emotion, and/or identity of the talker?

b. What speech movements were involved?

c. What phonemes, words, and/or sentences were these movements intended to represent?

d. What meaning do the phonemes/words/sentences carry?

e. What is the talker trying to accomplish?

When making these decisions, the listener does not have to rely only on the sensory evidence provided by his ears (and eyes, if watching a talker). The brain also receives evidence from the context. First, there is the physical context (the surroundings, other objects, other events). Second, if the event is someone talking, there is a social context (the people present, their relationships to each other and the listener) and a language context (phonemes are in words, words are in sentences, sentences are in conversation, narrative, etc.). Perceptual decisions are based on both kinds of evidence—sensory and contextual.

The ability to make full use of context requires prior knowledge (i.e., cognition). Knowledge determines how much of the potential information in the context can provide contextual evidence to the listener. Knowledge is also the source of possible decisions.

A Word About Recognition

We cannot recognize something about which we have no prior knowledge. Indeed, the word "recognition" literally means "knowing again."

The ability to interpret sound-making events also requires skill. Perceptual skill is not easily defined but includes such things as:

a. **Attention:** the ability to attend to the most relevant evidence and ignore the less relevant.

b. **Strategy:** the ability to reduce dependence on sensory evidence by taking full advantage of contextual evidence.

c. **Working memory:** the ability to retain partial evidence while waiting for more.

d. **Speed:** the ability to make decisions quickly, but not so quickly that too many mistakes are made.

e. **Adaptability:** the ability to adapt strategy to the demands of the listening situation.

Some of these skills may be innate. Others must be learned. Figure 3–6 offers a conceptual illustration of the process just described. Note that sensory and contextual evidence are what the brain receives. Knowledge and skills are what the listener brings to the task. Perceptual decisions are the result. The child with hearing loss is at a double disadvantage. The hearing loss not only reduces the amount of sensory evidence available for perceptual decision-making, it also interferes with the acquisition of the knowledge and skill needed to make use of this evidence.

A Word About Perceptual Speed

When we listen to speech, the speed at which we must make perceptual decisions is dictated by the talker—not by the listener. In this respect, listening to speech is different from reading text. A slow reader can still read successfully. But a slow listener fails if he can't keep up with the talker.

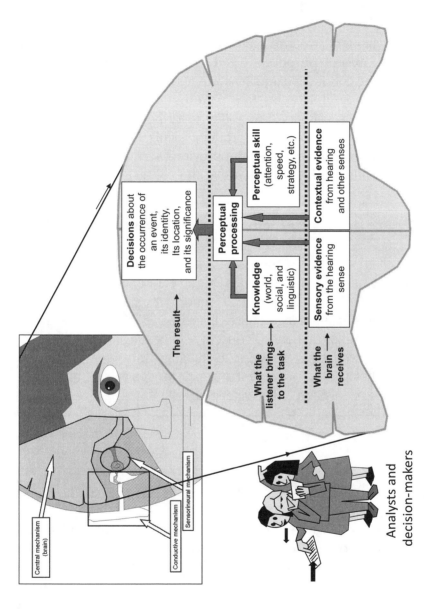

Central mechanism (brain)

Conductive mechanism

Sensorineural mechanism

Decisions about
the occurrence of
an event,
its identity,
Its location,
and its significance

The result →

Knowledge
(world,
social, and
linguistic)

Perceptual
processing

Perceptual skill
(attention,
speed,
strategy, etc.)

Sensory evidence
from the hearing
sense

Contextual evidence
from hearing
and other senses

What the
listener brings
to the task

What the
brain
receives

Analysts and
decision-makers

Figure 3–6. The central mechanism and the process of hearing.

Hearing Capacity and Hearing Skill

In later chapters, we will contrast hearing capacity and hearing skill. For present purposes, we define *hearing capacity* as the ability of the conductive and sensorineural mechanisms to convert patterns of sound stimulus into patterns of nerve impulses. This requires both sensitivity (the ability to respond to weak sounds) and resolution (the ability to reproduce detail). *Hearing skill*, on the other hand, was discussed in the previous section. It refers to the listener's ability to interpret sensory and contextual evidence.

Hearing Capacity, Skill, and Impairment

The child with hearing loss is at a double disadvantage. First, reduced hearing capacity limits the amount and quality of evidence provided to the brain. Second, the child has difficulty acquiring the knowledge and skill needed to interpret this evidence. We improve hearing capacity with hearing aids, cochlear implants, and other assistive technology. But we must also enrich the child's environment and experiences in ways that will promote acquisition of knowledge and skill.

Hearing With Two Ears

Decisions about where a sound came from are based mainly on differences between the patterns of nerve signals generated by the two ears. Hearing with two ears also helps us attend to one source of sound while ignoring others, and it helps reduce the interfering effects of noise. A loss of hearing in one ear is not catastrophic but it does represent a significant reduction of hearing capacity. By the same token, it is generally agreed that optimizing hearing capacity for a child with hearing loss requires assistance to both ears.

Some Things to Remember

1. **Hearing** depends on three mechanisms: the conductive mechanism, the sensorineural mechanism; and the central mechanism (the brain).

2. The **conductive** mechanism consists of the outer and middle ears. It collects sound and delivers it as efficiently as possible to the sensorineural mechanism.

3. The **sensorineural** mechanism consists of the cochlea and the auditory nerve. It translates sound stimuli into patterns of nerve impulses and sends them to the brain.

4. Within the cochlea, the conversion of sound stimuli into nerve impulses is the task of several thousand **hair cells** arrayed in four rows.

5. In the **central** mechanism (the brain), patterns of nerve impulses are analyzed, and decisions are made about the sound and the events that produced it.

6. **Decisions** in the brain are based on both the **sensory** evidence (coming from the cochlea) and **contextual** evidence.

7. The listener's **knowledge** (cognition) and **skill** determine the accuracy of perceptual decisions and the speed with which they are made.

8. Knowledge and skill depend almost entirely on **learning** and **experience**.

Relevance

Childhood hearing impairments can occur in any of the three hearing mechanisms. Knowledge of their different roles helps us understand the consequences and impact of different types of hearing loss, and the possibilities for management. Note also, the emphasis in this chapter on development and learning. Hearing aids and cochlear implants can reduce hearing loss but they do not restore normal hearing. To compensate for deficits in assisted hearing, we enrich the child's environment and experiences so as to optimize and speed the acquisition of the knowledge and skills on which the function of the central hearing mechanism depend. This is true for all aspects of hearing but it is especially true for those aspects related to spoken language.

To Learn More

■ Accessible information on this topic has long been available in *Hearing in Children* by Jerry Northern and Marion Downs, now in its 5th edition (Northern & Downs, 2002, Lippincott Williams and Wilkins, Baltimore: MD).

■ Comprehensive information for the more advanced student is provided by Stanley Gelfand in the 2004 (4th) edition of *Hearing: An Introduction to Psychological and Physiological Acoustics* (Gelfand, 2004).

CHAPTER 4

Hearing and Development

Nature provides the newborn with an assortment of capacities, and needs. Under normal circumstances, one of the capacities is hearing and one of the needs is communication. Nurture, in the form of the physical and social environment and the child's experiences, takes advantage of the hearing capacity and makes it possible for her to satisfy communicative needs with spoken language. In the process, the child develops the fine sensorimotor skills required for speech production and perception; she develops knowledge of the world to which language will refer; and she develops the knowledge of the world of people, and of herself, which will enable communication. These three functions—sensorimotor, cognitive, and social-emotional—provide the foundations for spoken language. For the child with hearing loss born into a hearing family, development of all three functions is at risk.

Stages of Development

Let us introduce you to Susan, born with normal sensory, motor, and learning capacities into a talking family who interact with her verbally and nonverbally during caretaking, play, and the activities of everyday living. Susan did not come into the world as an amorphous lump of clay waiting to be molded. Her anatomy was quite well developed and, by the time she was born, she also had some basic motor skills, mostly associated with breathing, feeding, and crying; some basic sensory capacities allowing reaction to physical stimuli; an amazing learning capacity; the foundations of an understanding of the physical and social worlds she had entered; and the foundations of an ability to interpret and reproduce facial features associated with emotions and speech. Most important, she came with a powerful drive to learn, and she finds herself in a physical and social environment that is ideally suited to promote learning. She is an eager student and the world is an ideal classroom.

As Susan learns and develops, she will pass through a series of stages. Within each stage, growth will be quantitative. She will do more of the same and do it better. The transition from one stage to the next, however, will be qualitative. She will do different things and do them differently. Walking, for example, is qualitatively different from crawling. This developmental process will be sequential, cumulative, directional, age-related, synchronous, adaptive, and mutual. What do we mean by these descriptors?

a. By "sequential," we mean that developmental stages will follow each other in an orderly sequence. Babbling will come before talking. Crawling will come before walking. But the stages will overlap. Susan will not abandon crawling as soon as she begins to walk. She will not abandon babbling as soon as she produces her first word.

b. By "cumulative," we mean that the skills developed during one stage of development are incorporated into a later stage. When she begins to talk, for example, she will be drawing on sensory and motor skills acquired during babbling.

c. By "directional," we mean that development moves toward a goal. The ultimate goal can be defined as an independent adult equipped to choose and pursue her own path to personal fulfillment. At any stage, however, the direction of development is largely driven by a desire for control. Susan will acquire control of her body (including the speech mechanism), of her location in space (crawling, walking, running), of objects (manipulation), and of people (ultimately by spoken language).

d. By "age-related," we mean that Susan will pass developmental milestones at fairly predictable ages. The schedule generally has been established through research in which the average and range of ages for emergence and/or mastery of specific skills are observed. Observations of language development have led to the concept of a "critical age" after which mastery is more difficult.

e. By "synchronous," we mean that parallel areas of development will be coordinated in time so that readiness skills in one area are in place when needs emerge in another. For example, basic hearing and speech skills will be ready when the need for language emerges.

f. By "adaptive," we mean that emerging skills and behaviors not only meet immediate needs but also prepare the way for needs that appear later. The opposite is "maladaptive," which occurs when skills and behaviors developed at one stage (such as successfully controlling parents through tantrums) stand in the way of developing appropriate skills and behaviors at a later stage (such as using language to negotiate with parents and express feelings).

g. By "mutual," we mean that Susan will influence her physical and social environments just as she is influenced by them. Think of the changes in Susan's home, and in her parents' roles, lifestyles, and self-images that will be prompted by the arrival of Susan, their first baby.

Susan's development, which actually began at conception, will be guided by interactions between genetically determined capacities and needs (nature) and the characteristics, demands, constraints, and reactions of her physical and social worlds (nurture). Development will be observed in several areas, including: sensory function; motor function; perception; knowledge and understanding of the world of things; knowledge and understanding of the world of people; awareness and management of the inner world of feelings; knowledge and use of language; intellectual attainment; and literacy.

More About Research on Child Development

Many names are associated with the early study of child development. Examples outside the United States include: Piaget, in Switzerland, who constructed theories and models of the ways in which children come to "know" their world; Vigotsky, in Russia,who explained cognitive development by describing the role that social interaction, and practices within the culture, play in the acquisition of knowledge; Freud, in Austria, who introduced the concepts of the unconscious mind and defense mechanisms; and Erikson, in Germany, who focused on the interdependence of nature and nurture. Work in the United States began in the Midwest within Home Economics departments of Agricultural Colleges and later spread to major universities. Important names include: Bruner and Skinner, at Harvard; Gesell, at Yale; Maslow, at Brandeis; Hilgard, at Stanford; Wellman, from Iowa; Furth, (eventually) from Washington, DC; and Parten, from Minnesota).

One of the problems faced by all researchers in this field is the limited opportunity for experiment. Empirical research involves several stages: observation; theories to explain the observations; predictions from those theories; experiments to test the predictions; and reconsideration of the theories based on the results. Much of the early work on child development, including the development of spoken language, stopped at the second stage—theories to explain observations. Ethical considerations and limited technology seriously restricted the kinds of experiment that could be done to test predictions based on these theories. In recent decades, however, researchers have devised ingenious tasks to explore the skills and beliefs of infants. The resulting observations have greatly enhanced our understanding of child development.

Sensorimotor Function

Sensory and motor development occur together, each dependent on the other. You can think of sensory development as the process by which the child learns to manage and organize the information that the brain receives from various senses. In addition to input from the six senses of touch, vision, hearing, balance, taste, and smell, the brain receives information from muscles, tendons, and joints. This last sense is known as proprioception, literally perception of one's self. It enables the child to learn about the positions, orientations, and movements of arms, legs, hands, feet, head, eyes, tongue, lips, and so on. A major aspect of sensory development is learning associations among the various senses. Touch, taste, and proprioception provide information via direct contact. Hearing, vision, and smell provide information from a distance—when things are too far away to reach and touch. Sensory development involves relating the two. One can think of vision and hearing as touching at a distance.

Motor development is the process by which the child learns to control the body and its various parts. This process is usually divided into gross-motor and fine-motor development. Gross-motor development leads to such skills as rolling over, sitting, crawling, standing, walking, running, jumping, throwing, and catching. Fine-motor development leads to such skills as manipulation of blocks, buttons, shoe laces, crayons, and other small objects. Of particular importance is development of fine-motor control of the speech mechanism. Note that the child comes into the world with several reflexive motor skills, including, breathing, sucking, swallowing, and crying. These skills provide a basis for later development of the fine motor control of the speech mechanism which, as pointed out in Chapter 2, is an adaptation of systems evolved for the more basic functions.

Sensory development and motor development do not occur independently. They are essential to each other. In order to control movement, the brain must have sensory input about the goal of the movement and sensory feedback about the results. The process also works in the other direction. In order to learn the significance of sensory input, the child must move and explore. One of the earliest examples of this interdependence occurs when the child moves her hand and watches the results. She learns that this object is under her control and, therefore, part of herself, and she begins to coordinate hand and eye. Later, the role of movement in sensory development becomes clear as the child explores the environment with hands and mouth—often to the consternation of the parents. Because of the interdependence of movement and the senses, this stage of development is appropriately referred to as *sensorimotor*. It is dominant during the first two years of life but can continue indefinitely. (Think of learning to play a musical instrument.)

Cognitive Function

Cognition is another word for "knowing." In this context, it applies to what the child "knows" about the world in which he lives. A special aspect of cognition is social cognition, which refers to what the child knows about that part of the world involving people. We are not talking, here, about explicit knowledge, as demonstrated in tests and quizzes. Rather, cognition refers to implicit knowledge. You know implicitly, for example, how to stand upright. But unless you are specially trained, you would be at a loss to explain the underlying relationships among gravity, base of support, balance, vision, and proprioception. Cognitive development refers to the process by which the child acquires knowledge of his world. It can be thought of as building an internal world model, based on information the brain receives from the senses both passively, by observation, and actively, by exploration.

Perceptual development is the first stage of cognitive development. In this stage, the child learns to interpret sensory information in terms of the specific objects, individuals, and events from which it originates. He also learns about the dimensions of space and time in which his world exists. Several subskills are involved in this process. One is selective attention. The child learns how to select, from an enormous amount of information, that which is relevant to the task at hand. Irrelevant information is relegated to the background. When applied to hearing, selective attention may be referred to as listening. Another perceptual subskill is monitoring. While attending to one source of information, the brain monitors the background in case something important happens. In this context, hearing is of particular importance for alerting to potentially significant events. Because it functions at a distance, in all directions, and remains operational during sleep, hearing is ideally suited to the role of watchdog.

Once a child has incorporated specific objects and events into his world model, he is able to recognize them (literally to re-cognize them, or to "know" them again). But recognition is no simple feat. Think, for a moment, about recognition through vision. Every time the child sees a particular toy, the pattern of light created on his retina is different. It changes with orientation, distance, and lighting, as illustrated in Figure 4–1. And yet, the child learns to extract the features that are reliably associated with that toy. He even learns that the toy remains a part of his world when it cannot be seen (object permanence). And he learns to recognize it when only a part is visible (object completion). If the toy makes noise, he will recognize it from hearing alone and if it has a characteristic odor, he will recognize it via his sense of smell. As indicated in Chapter 1, the properties of sound make hearing an ideal sense for recognizing events at a distance. Recognition of the event often leads to recognition of the objects involved, even when they cannot be seen. But the sound patterns generated by a given event (such as mother talking) are different every time it is experienced. Nevertheless, the child learns to extract those features of sound patterns (often referred to as *invariants*) that are reliably associated with the event. Perceptual development is dominant during the first two years of life but, like sensorimotor development, can continue indefinitely.

Figure 4–1. Pictures of a simple toy seen from different angles and distances and with different lighting. Same object—different sensory experiences.

In the case of hearing, perceptual development starts in the womb. The conductive and sensorineural mechanisms of hearing are fully functional at birth and the auditory pathways and brain centers are partially functional. Startle responses to loud sounds can occur before birth, and there is evidence to show that the melody and rhythm of the mother's speech are already imprinted on the unborn child's memory. Soon after birth, some directional hearing is apparent as the child turns her head toward a sound source. Alerting and listening are often exhibited by quieting or cessation of sucking. Once the child can sit unsupported at around

6 months of age, he will turn to look at the source of an interesting sound. Basically, hearing tells him that something happened (an event) and he uses vision to learn more about what it was and who or what was involved. The beginnings of sound recognition are exhibited by appropriate responses to such things as mother's voice, footsteps, and the sound of food preparation. As the child builds a perceptual model of his world, further associations develop between the objects and events in it and the resulting sound patterns. The resulting hearing skills will contribute to almost every other aspect of development.

Somewhere between 18 and 24 months of age, the child begins to organize the many objects, events, properties, and relationships of his developing world model conceptually. From the several specific balls he has observed, explored, used, and seen in use, he acquires the concept of "ball," as illustrated in Figure 4–2. The concept is not tied to a specific object but is a category that can hold all possible examples. Events also become organized conceptually. For example, from the many specific speech events he has heard, or engaged in, the child acquires the concept of "someone talking," a category that includes all possible instances of speech events but is not tied to any specific one. Similarly, the child acquires concepts of properties—shape, size, color, texture, number, wetness, and so on. And his experiences with space and time lead to spatial and temporal concepts such as near, far, on, in, behind, sudden, fast, slow, and future. Most importantly, the child develops the concept of causation. He learns that effects have causes and that the cause precedes the effect. The value of conceptual development cannot be overemphasized. It permits the creation of new categories for objects and events not previously encountered; it permits their subsequent recognition; it permits planning; and it permits the interpretation of events in terms of cause. Most importantly, it provides the foundation for language and communication. There can be no language without the conceptually organized world model to which it will refer. Other animals show evidence of rudimentary conceptual development, but none develop the range and complexity demonstrated by a 4-year-old child.

Figure 4–2. Pictures of different balls. Same concept—different instances.

Social-Emotional Function

We are social creatures. We live our lives in relationship to other people. At an early stage of evolution, the ability to function in groups of various sizes and compositions (family, clan, hunting party, etc.) provided increased security and improved food supply.

Because of the obvious benefits to survival and reproduction, a predisposition to interaction, communication, and cooperation is part of our genetic inheritance.

One aspect of the child's cognitive development involves learning about the objects in his environment, their properties, the events they are involved in, and the physical rules (or laws) by which they are governed. People, however, are a very special kind of object. In addition to their physical properties of size, color, and so forth, they have special properties, they are involved in special events, they are governed by special rules, and they exhibit special cause-effect relationships.

When social cognition reaches the stage of conceptual organization, a key result is the ability to imagine the world as experienced by another person. The child develops what is called a Theory of Mind. Numerous experiments have demonstrated modifications in a child's behavior based on what he believes another person to have perceived. This ability is fundamental to communication—one aspect of which is the deliberate creation of sensory stimuli with the goal of influencing another.

Babies experience many emotions: comfort, discomfort, anger, fear, anxiety, loneliness, pleasure, pride, and so on. The immediate stimuli are internal but the resulting sensations may become associated with objects or events in the environment. For example, the mother and her actions become associated with positive emotions of comfort and pleasure, plus the relief from negative emotions such as hunger and loneliness. There are also some instinctive associations. It is typical, for example, for children to show wariness or fear of strangers between 7 and 12 months of age. Toddlers demonstrate joy in mastery. True pride, however, is a self-evaluative emotion and is expressed more fully by preschoolers who are beginning to compare themselves to an internal standard of performance.

The inclusion of emotions in the conceptual organization of his experience, along with the evolving theory of mind, allows the child to make inferences about another person's emotional reactions to a situation. He is in a position to empathize. This development also allows the child to use communication as a way to intentionally affect the emotional state of another, for better or worse.

Like every other object in the child's evolving world model, "self" comes with a variety of properties. Positive self-assessments such as "valued by others," "interesting to be with," and "capable of solving problems" can be assumed to promote exploration, interaction, and communication. In the early stages of development, these usually can be taken for granted. But once the child acquires the ability to imagine other people's perceptions and sense their emotional reactions, his self-image will be influenced by their reactions to him. Fortunately, the instinctive reactions of most parents to the normally developing child support the maintenance of a positive and realistic self-image.

Spoken Language Acquisition

The three areas of development just summarized provide the basis for language development, as illustrated in Figure 4–3:

a. Sensorimotor development allows the child to perceive and produce the sound patterns that will be the building blocks of spoken language.

b. Cognitive development provides her with the world model to which language can refer.

c. Social-emotional development provides her with the impetus and skills for communication with other people.

As the child experiments with language as a tool for communication, the result becomes aligned with the language already being used in the environment; the child learns, acquires, or recreates the language of his social and cultural environment. The normally hearing child, born into a talking family, acquires spoken language. The deaf child, born into a signing family, develops signed language. Our immediate concern is the deaf child who is born into a talking family. Hearing loss weakens or removes the sensorimotor basis for his acquisition of spoken language. The hearing deficit can also undermine the cognitive and social-emotional bases.

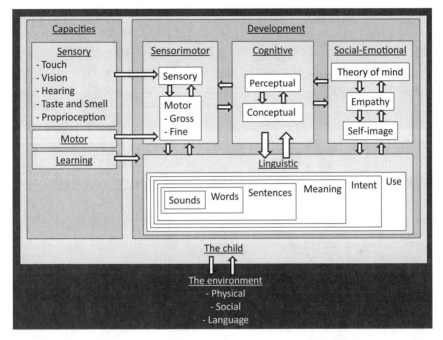

Figure 4–3. Sensory, motor, and learning capacities provide the basis for child development (nature). Sensorimotor development leads to management and control of sensory input and movement. Cognitive development begins perceptually, with the specific, and progresses conceptually to the general. Of special importance is social cognition, which contributes to social-emotional development. Sensorimotor, cognitive, and social-emotional function provide the three foundations for spoken language. Their development depends on interactions with the physical and social environment (nurture).

As already indicated, cognitive development results in an internal world model. It is this model to which language will refer when used for communication. The world model and the language used to refer to it are inseparable, like two sides of a coin. Without cognition, there can be no language. A key feature of child development, however, is that language, once acquired, becomes a powerful tool for further cognitive development. This is a beautiful example of positive feedback by which effects enhance their own causes. Once a child has acquired some competence, she can expand and refine her world model through language. She is no longer tied to direct physical exploration as a tool for cognitive development. Language frees cognitive development from the here and now. And the more she learns, the more advanced her language becomes. In an engineering context, positive feedback is a bad thing. It causes runaway vibrations in such things as buildings, bridges, and airplanes, leading to collapse. In hearing aids, it leads to constant whistling. In a child between the ages of 2 and 4, however, positive feedback is a good thing. It leads to runaway cognitive and linguistic development as the two feed on each other. Positive feedback is also observed in the other two bases of language development. Talking leads to refinement of the underlying production and perception skills on which it depends. Communication enhances the underlying social-emotional status on which it depends. Many such feedback loops are illustrated by the two-directional arrows in Figure 4–3. The most dramatic one, however, is that connecting cognition and language. Cognition leads to language, which enhances cognition, which leads to more language, and so on. The explosion in these two areas of development between the ages of 2 and 4 is truly phenomenal.

As the child develops spoken language, she must acquire competence at many nested levels, as illustrated in Figure 4–3:

a. **Phonology.** The child must learn to recognize and produce the sound patterns of the language being used by the people around her. These patterns are of two types: (1) *segments* (vowels and consonants) that are combined in overlapping sequences to create syllables, words, and sentences, and (2) *suprasegmentals* such as melody and rhythm that apply to these sequences (see Chapter 2).

b. **Vocabulary.** The child's evolving world model must be organized into conceptual categories and he must develop word labels with which to reference them. At first, the words will refer to specific objects and events. Later, they will refer to conceptual categories. At this point, the label, by itself, is no longer specific, but can become specific when used in a sentence.

More About Words

The child's evolving world model exists in space and time, both of which have attributes. Space is occupied by objects and materials which also have attributes. Objects and materials become involved in events, which occupy time. These events have attributes. Objects and events also have spatial and temporal relationships. The evolving vocabulary reflects this model. Nouns refer to categories of objects and materials (ball, man, water). Adjectives refer to properties of objects and materials (green, big, wet). Verbs refer to categories of events (wash, eat, hit). Adverbs refer to properties of events (slow, sudden, angry), and also to properties of properties (very, extremely, slightly). Prepositions refer to spatial and temporal relationships (in, behind, before, after). This is just one example of the intimate relationship between the world model and the language model that is used both to refer to it and to externalize it for purposes of communication.

c. **Sentences.** Sentences express meaning. A sentence can consist of a single word (e.g., "tea?") when used to mean, "Do you want tea?" but more typically consists of a sequence of words. Each language has a *grammar* (or *syntax*), which is a system of rules for selecting, modifying, and sequencing words. For example, the general labels "chair," "dirt," "blue," and "is" can be modified and combined into, "The blue chair is dirty." Our developing child must learn these rules.

d. **Meaning** is used, here, to describe the surface message. The relationships between words or sentences and their meaning are usually discussed under the heading of **semantics**.

e. **Intent** is used, here, to describe the talker's purpose in expressing the surface meaning. For example, the sentence, "The blue chair is dirty" with its simple surface meaning may carry an intent more accurately expressed as, "Clean the blue chair" or "I don't want to sit in a dirty chair."

f. **Pragmatics** is being used, here, to refer to the child's ability to create messages with meanings that will satisfy intent. It also includes knowledge of the social rules of interaction and conversation. Note that the principal use of language is to control another person. Through *narrative,* we control another's knowledge ("Bobby hit me!"). Through *question,* we control another's speech ("where's Daddy?"). Through *request,* we control another's action ("stop it!"). Most sentences belong to one of these three categories.

When analyzed in this way, the task of acquiring spoken language competence seems formidable. But young children accomplish it in a few years and without apparent effort.

Timetable

So what do we expect for Susan? Reflexive vocalization will begin at birth but, by 4 to 6 weeks Susan will begin to differentiate her vocalizations to signal hunger, pain, and discomfort. As caregivers respond differently to different cries, she will further differentiate and explore her vocalizations with the discovery that she has control of people. At this time, the sounds will have little to do with those she hears. Babbling will start around 3 months of age when Susan begins to hone her sounds to match the patterns she hears. Because her parents respond to her babbling, she will also begin to develop the timed interactions and turn-taking that will underlie later conversational competence. Susan's first word will appear at around 1 year of age. We will know it is a word rather than a chance combination of sounds, because she will use it in relation to a certain person, object, or activity. At this time, she will be using speech for communication but complex messages will be encapsulated in one word—usually with a very specific meaning (e.g., "up," "juice"). Around 18 months, Susan will start to combine words to express meanings that rely on the relationships among the words. Emergence of this process will also signal transition to conceptual organization of her world model. Between 2 and 4 years of age, Susan's world model and vocabulary will grow exponentially. At the same time, she will be learning the rules for making meaningful sentences. During this period, she will often overgeneralize rules she has learned ("I eated it"), but will correct these "errors" over time. By 4 years of age, Susan will be a highly competent user of language. In the next few years, she will perfect her speech production, correct a few remaining errors in grammar, learn more about using language to satisfy intent, and greatly expand her world model and vocabulary. But the rate of growth will be slow compared with the explosion between 2 and 4 years.

The role of hearing in this process is paramount. At every stage, it plays a key role. Hearing provides Susan with access to the sound patterns of language as produced by the people around her. Through hearing, she learns to control her own speech mechanism and to imitate those sound patterns. During perceptual development, hearing is associated with every other way of experiencing objects, people, and events, especially the events that she herself generates—hitting crib toys, banging with a spoon, playing with blocks, splashing the bath water, and so on. When she organizes her world model conceptually, hearing provides her with access to the words and sentences used by the people in her environment as they talk to her and to each other. Hearing makes it possible for her to communicate verbally. The resulting competence with spoken language has a profound influence on subsequent cognitive, social-emotional, and communicative development.

Some Things to Remember

1. The newborn child comes with a basic **repertoire** of sensory and motor skills, an enormous learning capacity, a powerful drive to learn, and the foundations of an understanding of the worlds of things and people.

2. Development occurs by **interaction** among these skills, capacities, and drives (nature) and the physical and social environment (nurture).

3. During **sensorimotor** development, the child learns how to organize, manage, and control sensory input and motor output.

4. During **cognitive** development, the child builds an internal model of the world—at first perceptual and later conceptual.

5. During **social-emotional** development, the child builds that part of her world model involving people—and herself.

6. **Spoken language** acquisition depends on the foregoing three factors:

   a. Sensorimotor development leads to the necessary hearing and speech skills,

   b. Cognitive development provides the world model to which language refers, and

   c. Social-emotional development provides the drive and basis for communication.

7. **Positive feedback** is evident when language is used to enhance the world model to which it refers—accounting, in part, for the rapid explosion of cognition and language between the ages of 2 and 4 years.

8. **Hearing** plays a key role at every stage of normal development.

Relevance

Hearing loss obviously threatens the auditory component of sensorimotor development. It also limits the child's ability to hear the spoken language of others and to produce speech. If hearing loss is the child's only impairment, all other aspects of development will proceed according to plan until it is time for the explosive interaction between cognition and language. At this point, without intervention, the result is likely to be maladaptive development. The first step in intervention is to ensure that hearing capacity is as good as it can be. But modern hearing aids and cochlear implants, sophisticated as they are, cannot restore normal hearing. The second step in intervention is to ensure that hearing skills are as good as they can be, given the limitation of assisted hearing. The third step is to ensure optimal cognitive, social-emotional, and spoken language development, with hearing playing as much of a role as it can. The second and third steps are accomplished by enriching the child's physical and social environments and experiences. Much of this is done indirectly through instruction, counseling, and coaching of family and caregivers. Once the child is in preschool, additional direct intervention is possible. In all of this work, a solid understanding of the many facets of child development is important. An exclusive focus on hearing, listening skills, and speech is in danger of ignoring the need for optimal cognitive and social-emotional development as foundations for spoken language development and communicative competence. We will explore these issues further when we discuss management in Part 2 of this text.

To Learn More

■ We recommend *The Scientist in the Crib: What Early Learning Tells Us About the Mind* by Gopnik, Meltzoff, and Kuhl (2001). This is a very readable account of recent research on cognitive and linguistic development in infants. The title has two meanings, one of which serves to draw a parallel between the scientific method of observation, theory, prediction, test, and revision, and the exploratory processes engaged in by the developing child as he builds an internal model of the physical and social worlds in which he finds himself.

■ For additional reading, we suggest *NurtureShock: New Thinking About Children* by Bronson and Merryman

(2009). As the title suggests, this book emphasizes the key role of the child's environment and experiences in development.

■ After 40 years, Hans Furth's *Piaget for Teachers* still provides a valuable account of the work of one of the more influential researchers on child development (Furth, 1970).

■ For comprehensive coverage of the topic, there are several textbooks. We suggest exploring *Child Development: A Practitioner's Guide* (3rd ed.) (Davies, 2011) or *Child Development* (8th ed.) (Berk, 2008).

CHAPTER 5

Hearing Impairment and Hearing Loss

Overview

In previous chapters, we discussed hearing in terms of its nature, its anatomy, the process, and its role in development—especially of spoken language. We now turn to what can go wrong. Hearing can be impaired in many ways. If there is a reduction of sensitivity, which can be measured in decibels, we refer to the impairment as a hearing loss. Impairments can occur in any part of the hearing mechanism. If the conductive mechanism is affected, we refer to a conductive hearing loss. Such losses are never complete, they can be temporary, and they are often treatable with medicine or surgery. If the cochlea and its nerve connections are affected, we refer to a sensorineural hearing loss. Such losses can be total, they are usually permanent, and they cannot be cured with medicine or surgery. If the central mechanism is impaired, there may or not be a decibel hearing loss. There will, however, be problems with the interpretation of sound. These three kinds of impairment can occur in isolation or in combination. The potential impact of a hearing impairment on development can depend, among other things, on its type and location, its degree in decibels, and the age it was acquired. The focus in this text is on children with sensorineural hearing loss born to hearing parents. Over 90% of children with serious sensorineural hearing loss fall into this category, and their parents usually want their child to become competent in spoken language. Most of what we have to say in Part 2 of this text will assume that hearing loss is the only impairment affecting development. In reality, however, some 30% of children with sensorineural hearing loss are likely to have one or more additional impairments that complicate management.

Impairment and Loss

The term *hearing impairment* is used, here, in a general sense, to refer to any defect of the hearing mechanisms. The defect can be in the conductive mechanism, the sensorineural mechanism, or the central mechanism. The term *hearing loss* is used when there is a shift in the threshold of hearing, that is, a loss of sensitivity. The degree of hearing loss is expressed in decibels. This number tells us how much stronger than normal a sound must be in order to be heard. Impairments of conductive or sensorineural mechanisms produce a hearing loss. Impairments of the central mechanism may or may not.

Conductive Impairment

Conductive impairments occur when the outer and middle ears fail to deliver sound efficiently to the cochlea, as illustrated in Figure 5–1.

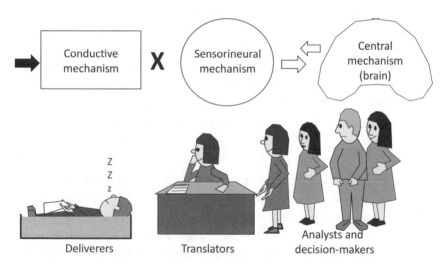

Figure 5–1. Conductive hearing impairment occurs when the conductive mechanism fails to deliver sound efficiently to the sensorineural mechanism.

Causes include such things as blockage of the ear canal, perforation of the eardrum, and breakage or fixation of the ossicular chain. The most common cause of conductive hearing loss in children is inflammation or infection of the middle ear (otitis media).

Conductive impairment produces a hearing loss. It does not, however, affect the clarity of sounds that are strong enough to be heard. Moreover, the loudness of the sound sensation grows with increasing amplitude of the sound stimulus at a normal rate.

More About Otitis Media

Otitis media usually begins with failure of the eustachian tube to ventilate the middle ear cavity. As air in the cavity is absorbed, the eardrum is pushed inward and can no longer vibrate freely. If the condition persists, the air in the cavity is replaced with a watery fluid, further restricting vibration of the eardrum. If bacteria grow in the fluid, the body sends white blood cells to kill them, resulting in the formation of pus. As the amount of pus grows, the eardrum is forced outward and may well rupture. Delay in treatment can result in a permanent conductive hearing loss from scarring, erosion of the ossicles, or eardrum perforation. Even if there is no permanent hearing loss, frequent recurrence can result in an impairment of auditory processing, leading to language and learning delays.

If the conductive mechanism is totally ineffective, sound can still reach the cochlea by direct vibration of the skull. For this reason, conductive hearing loss is never total. In extreme cases, it can be as high as 60 dB but is seldom higher than 45 dB. Conductive impairments often can be eliminated with medical or surgical intervention, and middle ear infections often resolve themselves without intervention. If a conductive loss is permanent, hearing aids can overcome the loss of sensitivity. Because there is no disturbance of loudness or loss of clarity, hearing aids are usually well accepted and very effective. Children with conductive loss are not candidates for cochlear implants.

Sensorineural Impairment

Sensorineural impairments occur when the sensorineural mechanism fails to translate patterns of sound into patterns of nerve activation as efficiently as it should (Figure 5–2). Causes can include loss of hair cells in the cochlea, poor connections between hair cells and nerve fibers (sometimes known as *auditory dissynchrony*), and damage to the nerve fibers themselves (sometimes known as *auditory neuropathy*). The most common cause in children is an inherited genetic weakness. Another cause is meningitis, in which bacteria or viruses invade the cochlea and damage or destroy hair cells. Lack of oxygen during the birth process can also damage hair cells.

Sensorineural impairments produce a hearing loss. Unlike conductive impairments, however, they are also likely to produce a loss of clarity in the sounds that are strong enough to be heard. In other

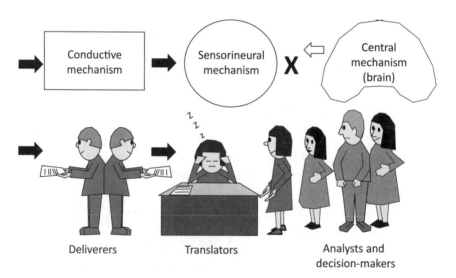

Figure 5–2. Sensorineural hearing impairment occurs when the sensorineural mechanism fails to translate sound into patterns of nerve activation as efficiently as it should.

words, some of the detail in the sound stimulus is missing from the sound sensation. Moreover, once a sound is above threshold, loudness of the sound sensation tends to grow unusually rapidly with increasing amplitude. This phenomenon is known as recruitment of loudness, or just *recruitment*. It can create a situation in which the person with sensorineural impairment experiences the same loudness from high amplitude sounds as the person with normal hearing, even though he cannot hear weak sounds.

Because there is no other way for sound sensations to reach the brain, sensorineural losses can be total. Moreover, the impairment itself cannot be eliminated with medical or surgical intervention. Hearing aids can overcome the loss of sensitivity but disturbances of loudness and loss of clarity can affect acceptance and effectiveness. In extreme cases, the benefit of hearing aids can be very small or even nonexistent. In such cases, cochlear implants are often an effective alternative. The surgery involved in cochlear implantation does not eliminate the impairment, but it does provide an alternative way for the brain to receive information about sound. Figure 5–3 serves as a reminder of the differences between conductive and sensorineural hearing loss.

Conductive and sensorineural hearing loss: some differences

Conductive hearing loss	Sensorineural hearing loss
• Never greater than 60 dB • Clarity is normal when sounds are loud enough • Loudness grows normally with increasing decibels • Often temporary • Often cured by surgery • Benefit from hearing aids is usually high • Cochlear implant is never appropriate	• Can be total • Clarity is reduced, even when sounds are loud enough • Loudness may grow suddenly with increasing decibels • Usually permanent • Cannot be cured by surgery • Benefit from hearing aids is sometimes limited • Cochlear implant is sometimes appropriate

Figure 5–3. Contrasting conductive and sensorineural impairment.

Central Impairment

There are situations in which the parts of the brain responsible for attending to, interpreting, and making decisions about patterns of nerve activation generated by the sensorineural mechanism fail to function properly, as illustrated in Figure 5–4. The impairment can be specific to hearing, in which case we may refer to an *auditory processing disorder*. Alternatively, it can be part of a more general problem of sensory or language processing. There can be actual physical damage or the problem can be one of organization. There may or may not be a loss of sensitivity. The problem can exist in isolation or it can occur in combination with a conductive or sensorineural hearing loss.

At this point we must distinguish between auditory processing *disorders* and ongoing auditory *development*. Many of the skills

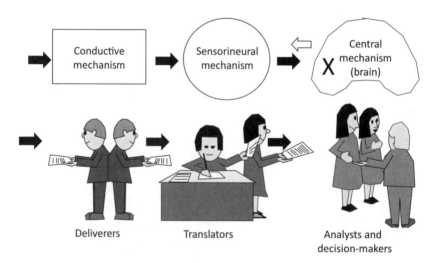

Figure 5–4. Central hearing impairment occurs when the brain centers responsible for hearing do not adequately attend to, or interpret, messages from the sensorineural mechanism.

involved in attending to and interpreting sound are learned. In a child with normal conductive and sensorineural mechanisms, a failure to learn may be evidence of a structural or organizational disorder. In a child with a conductive or peripheral loss, however, delays in the development of listening skills are to be expected. One goal of management is to reduce these delays by enriching meaningful listening experience.

Degree of Hearing Loss

As indicated earlier, degree of hearing loss is expressed in decibels. The number tells us how much stronger than normal a sound must be before the individual can detect it. Hearing loss varies across frequency and between ears. If, therefore, we measure a child's hearing loss in both ears at six or seven frequencies, we end up with 12 or 14 numbers. To reduce this information, we usually express the hearing loss of an ear as the average of the hearing loss at three frequencies: 500, 1000, and 2000 Hz. This choice is based on the fact that these three frequencies fall in the range of most importance to speech perception. The number is referred to as the three-frequency pure-tone average (or PTA) loss. But this still leaves us with two numbers, one for the right ear and one for the left. The impact of the hearing loss on the child's development will depend mainly on the hearing in the better ear, that is, the one with the lower hearing loss. If, therefore, we want a single number for the severity of a child's hearing loss, we choose the three-frequency average of the better ear. A child with a 100 decibel loss in the right ear and a 50 decibel loss in the left, for example, would be said to have a hearing loss of 50 dB. If, however, a child has normal hearing in one ear and a 100 dB loss in the other, we do not say he has a 0 dB loss. Instead we would say he has a unilateral (or one-sided) 100 dB hearing loss. We *never* use the average of the two ears when expressing a child's hearing loss with a single number.

Labeling Hearing Loss

As experience was accumulated in the 19th and 20th centuries, educators and clinicians began to categorize sensorineural hearing loss in terms of its impact on the development of spoken language. Thus, a "mild" hearing loss would have only a mild effect; a "moderate" hearing loss would have a moderate effect; and so on. With the development of pure-tone audiometry, it became possible to relate these labels to degree of hearing loss in decibels. The labels were applied to an ear (e.g., John has a severe hearing loss in the left ear and a profound hearing loss in the right), or to a child (e.g., John is severely deaf). Two things have happened to these labels. First, the descriptors lost much of their relevance in the face of developments in early intervention, hearing-aid technology, and cochlear implants. Second, audiologists adopted the labels as replacements for numbers, regardless of frequency (e.g., John's right ear shows a moderate hearing loss in the low frequencies falling to a profound hearing loss above 1000 Hz). Because these labels are used in audiological reports, it is helpful for parents, teachers, and clinicians to know how they relate to threshold.

Mild	25 to 40 dB
Moderate	41 to 55 dB
Moderately severe	55 to 70 dB
Severe	71 to 90 dB
Profound	greater than 90 dB

When applied to a child's better-ear three-frequency pure-tone average threshold, these labels can still have meaning in terms of unassisted hearing. *Without a hearing aid or cochlear implant,* a child with a severe hearing loss can hear her own speech but not that of other people at conversational distance. A child with a profound loss cannot even hear her own speech. In neither case will the child develop spoken language without appropriate intervention.

Age at Acquisition

One of the most important factors influencing the developmental implications of hearing loss is the age at which it was acquired. Cognitive, auditory, and language development begin at birth (if not before). Any development that has taken place before a hearing loss is acquired serves to reduce the impact of the loss and increase the effectiveness of intervention. The most dramatic difference is between children who acquire hearing loss before establishing spoken language skills and those who acquire it afterward. Developments in early identification, early intervention, and sensory management have blurred this distinction but the categorization can still be meaningful.

a. **Congenital:** This means that the hearing loss was present at birth. Little or no prior auditory or language development can be assumed. Notice that "congenital" does *not* mean "genetic." It is about time of acquisition, not cause.

b. **Prelingual:** Acquisition between 0 and 2 years of age. Rapid vocabulary growth has not begun although some auditory and basic language skills may be in place. Note, however, that "prelingual" includes "congenital."

c. **Perilingual:** Acquisition between 2 and 4 years of age. The child becomes deaf while in the period of rapid development of vocabulary and syntax.

d. **Postlingual:** Acquisition after 4 years of age. Basic syntax and vocabulary are fairly well developed.

Other age-related issues include the length of time between acquisition and identification of hearing loss and between acquisition of the loss and the provision of intervention, especially the provision of hearing aids or cochlear implants. The general rule, here, is: the sooner the better.

Causes

Causes of hearing impairment usually fall into one of four categories:

1. **Genetics:** The child inherits a genetic weakness which causes the hearing mechanism to develop imperfectly, or without adequate protection from other insults. There are well over a hundred genes involved in the development and function of the hearing mechanism and a defect in any one of them can cause hearing impairment

More About Inherited Deafness

We usually classify inheritance into two categories:

Dominant inheritance: This requires only one defective gene from one parent. The child has at least one deaf parent and had a 50% chance of inheriting the condition.

Recessive inheritance: This requires two identical defective genes, one from each parent. The child's parents have normal hearing but both are carriers of the same defective gene. Often, there is a family relationship between the parents. The child had a 25% chance of inheriting two copies of the defective gene and having a hearing impairment. He had a 50% chance of inheriting only one defective gene, in which case he would not have had the hearing impairment but could pass that gene on to the next generation.

Note that dominant inheritance is not common. Some 90 to 95% of deaf children have two parents with normal hearing.

2. **Infection:** Bacteria or viruses invade the auditory mechanism and cause damage. The most common example is meningitis. Infection of the mother during pregnancy can also cause hear-

ing impairment in the child, the most famous example being an epidemic of German measles (rubella) in the 1960s.

3. **Drugs:** The hair cells are particularly sensitive to certain drugs. A well-known example is streptomycin which may be used to treat life-threatening condition.

4. **Trauma:** Physical damage to the hearing mechanism can occur from such things as head injury, excessive noise, and oxygen deprivation. Impairments resulting from premature birth can be considered a form of trauma.

Other Issues

Our main concern in this text is with children who have sensori-neural hearing loss. Such children, however, are just as likely to experience middle ear infections as are children with normal hearing. In fact, the identification and treatment of middle ear infections may well be delayed because the early effects are masked by the sensorineural loss. Persistent middle ear infections can have two serious consequences. In children who use hearing aids, the additional 30 or 40 dB hearing loss can render the aid temporarily useless. The child must, essentially, function without hearing for the duration of the infection. Second, unable to trust hearing, the brain is likely to demote that sense from its key role as the watchdog sense and the primary source of information about speech. In other words, the child's problems can become compounded by deficits of alerting and attention. Parents, teachers, and clinicians need to be on the lookout for signs of impending ear infections and to pursue treatment promptly.

The last point about attention deficits resulting from intermittent conductive disorders highlights the interdependence of conductive, sensorineural, and central functions. By limiting the information supplied to the brain, a sensorineural or conductive impairment can slow and impede development of skills and knowledge required for central processing (see Figure 3–6). Moreover, the relationship can function in both directions. There is increasing evidence that information from the central mechanisms feeds back to the sensorineural system, refining its function as an efficient translator from the language of sound to the language of the brain.

Roughly one-third of children with hearing impairments have additional disorders. Such disorders can have serious effects on cognition, listening skills, the incorporation of hearing into development, and the effectiveness of intervention. Teachers and clinicians need to be aware of the presence of such disorders, to assess their impact, and be prepared to adapt their intervention strategies accordingly.

The loss of clarity associated with sensorineural hearing impairment tends to increase with degree of hearing loss in decibels, but the relationship is by no means perfect. Two children with the same degree of hearing loss can have very different abilities when it comes to the translation of sound patterns into patterns of neural activation. We can use degree of hearing loss as a guide to expectations but we should base decisions about intervention on emerging results.

The emergence of cochlear implants as a viable option for children with very severe, profound, or total hearing loss has revolutionized the management of childhood deafness. For the implanted child, auditory ability is determined by how well the implant can translate patterns of sound into patterns of electric current flow and how well the patterns of electric current flow can generate patterns of nerve activation. This ability has little or nothing to do with the severity of the initial hearing loss. In fact, some totally deaf children, with the aid of a cochlear implant, function as well as children with moderate hearing loss who wear hearing aids. The cochlear implant has rendered degree of hearing loss virtually irrelevant as a guide to management and expectations.

Finally, recall that 90 to 95% of children with a hearing loss of sufficient severity to prevent the spontaneous development of spoken language are born into hearing families. For these families, the child's acquisition of spoken language competence is usually a primary goal. With early identification, effective sensory management, and appropriate intervention, this goal generally is attainable.

Some Things to Remember

1. Hearing can be impaired because of several types of **cause**: genetics, infection, drugs, or trauma.

2. The term **hearing impairment** is used, here, in a generic sense whereas **hearing loss** is quantitative, referring to a decibel shift in threshold.

3. **Conductive impairment** affects the delivery of a sound stimulus to the cochlea. It reduces sound sensitivity but not sound clarity. Conductive impairments can be temporary and, if not, can often be fixed by medical or surgical treatment.

4. **Sensorineural impairment** affects the translation of sound stimuli into sound sensations. It reduces both sensitivity and clarity and cannot be eliminated by medical or surgical treatment. (It may, however, be amenable to surgical intervention in the form of cochlear implantation.)

5. **Central impairment** disrupts the interpretation of sensory evidence and is not amenable to medical or surgical treatment. It may, however, respond to other forms of therapeutic intervention.

6. The **developmental consequences** of sensorineural hearing loss, without appropriate intervention, are highly dependent on degree of loss and age at acquisition.

7. Ninety to 95% of deaf children have **hearing parents.**

8. Thirty to 40% of deaf children have one or more **additional impairments** that exacerbate the developmental consequences of hearing impairment and increase the challenges of intervention.

Relevance

The type of impairment, the degree of hearing loss, the age at acquisition, and the presence of additional impairments are all factors that influence the developmental implications of hearing impairment. They also affect management choices. An understanding of these issues is important to the development of intervention strategies that are matched to individual needs. In addition, it is especially important for parents and professionals to realize that a child with sensorineural hearing loss can still get middle ear infections which will add to the decibel hearing loss until they are resolved.

To Learn More

- There are many texts dealing with hearing impairment and hearing loss. A thorough treatment is provided in the opening chapters of *Pediatric Audiology*, edited by Madell and Flexer (2008).

- Chapter 1 of this text, by Stach and Ramachandran, deals specifically with hearing disorders in children.

- Chapter 2, by Rehm and Madore, focuses on the genetics of hearing loss.

- For a more basic treatment, we suggest relevant sections of *Your Child's Hearing Loss: A Guide for Parents* by Waldman and Roush (2009).

CHAPTER 6

Hearing Tests

Overview

In this chapter we discuss hearing tests and their implications for intervention. As indicated in the previous chapter, pure-tone audiometry measures an individual's threshold of hearing for several pure tones. The result is an *audiogram* in which threshold is expressed in relation to normal. The audiogram shows the child's hearing loss for sounds that are delivered to the ear canal. By repeating the test with sounds sent directly to the cochlea, using a vibrator attached to the skull, we can differentiate conductive from sensorineural loss. Adding the speech banana (see Chapters 1 and 2) to the audiogram, helps us to estimate how much of the useful information the child can hear in the sounds of conversational speech. Threshold testing requires a response to indicate that sound stimuli are being converted to sound sensations. The choice of response is based on the age and developmental level of the child. In addition to behavioral methods, one can use brain waves to determine when the threshold of hearing has been reached. Pure-tone audiometry is only the most basic hearing test. Other tests provide information about such things as the condition of the conductive and sensorineural mechanisms and about the clarity of sound sensations. The results of hearing tests are used in planning intervention and evaluating progress.

Pure-Tone Audiogram

Let us introduce you to Simon. He is 18 months old and has a hearing loss. Figure 6–1 shows his *pure-tone audiogram,* which was obtained during his first full audiologic evaluation. To Simon's

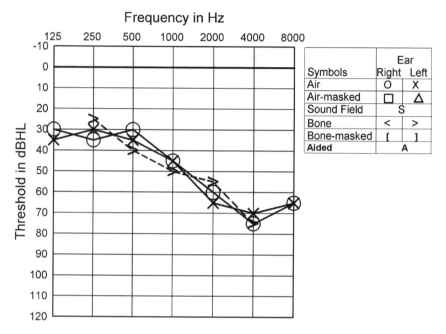

Figure 6–1. Simon's pure-tone audiogram.

parents, this chart is, at first, as informative as a runic inscription. It doesn't take much explanation, however, to unlock its mysteries.

Note, first, that threshold testing seeks to find the lowest decibel level, relative to normal, at which a sound stimulus produces a sound sensation. In other words, we determine the quietest sound the individual can hear. This quantity is called the *hearing threshold* and is express in dBHL. The HL stands for Hearing Level. If the hearing were normal, the thresholds would be along the zero line, at 0 dBHL.

In pure-tone testing, threshold is determined for tones at several frequencies, using 5 dB amplitude steps. The results can be written down but are usually plotted on an audiogram form, as in Figure 6–1. Various symbols are used to indicate how the sound was delivered and to which ear. The basic method of presentation is via the air in the ear canal. The process is known as *air-conduction testing* and the results are *air-conduction thresholds*. The Os and Xs show air-conduction thresholds for the right and left ears, respectively. This distinction, however, assumes that earphones were used. If sound is delivered by a loudspeaker it is never clear which ear responded and the Os and Xs would be replaced by "S" for sound-field. The symbols joined by the dashed line show *bone-conduction thresholds*. These thresholds are obtained by *bone-conduction testing* in which sound is delivered directly to the cochlea by a vibrator placed behind the ear. The main purpose of bone-conduction testing is to determine how much of the hearing impairment is sensorineural and how much is conductive. In Simon's case the absence of a significant difference between air- and bone-conduction thresholds indicates that the loss is sensorineural.

More About Bone-Conduction Testing

In air-conduction testing, sound must travel through the conductive mechanism before reaching the sensorineural mechanism. Air-conduction thresholds, therefore, show the combined effect of any conductive loss and any sensorineural loss. If there are both kinds (a mixed loss) the two losses will add together. Bone-conduction testing, however, bypasses the conductive mechanism. As a result, a bone-conduction threshold shows only the effect of any sensorineural loss. Any difference between the air-and bone-conduction thresholds (referred to as an air-bone-gap) must be the result of a conductive loss. In Simon's case, there is no significant air-bone gap and we conclude that the loss is sensorineural. For clarification, Figure 6–2 shows audiograms for ears with sensorineural, conductive, and mixed hearing losses. Remember:

1. Air-conduction threshold measures sensorineural plus conductive loss.

2. Bone-conduction threshold measures sensorineural loss alone.

3. The difference between the two (the air-bone- gap) measures conductive loss alone.

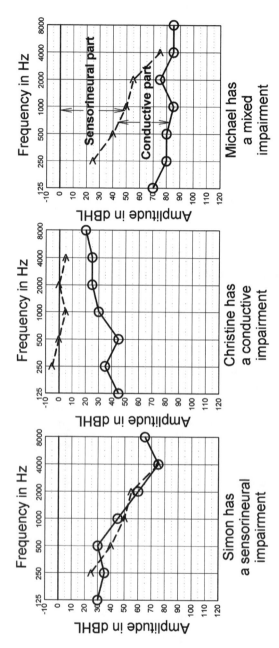

Figure 6–2. Audiograms showing the value of bone-conduction testing.

84

Lost and Surviving Hearing

Figure 6–3 shows the air-conduction thresholds for Simon's right ear. The heavy line encloses the area of Simon's hearing in which tones are strong enough to be heard but not so strong as to cause discomfort (see Chapter 1). The threshold line divides the area of normal hearing into two parts. The upper part is the area of *lost hearing*. Simon cannot hear tones in his right ear if their frequencies and amplitudes place them in this area. The lower part is the area of *surviving hearing*. Simon can hear tones in his right ear if their frequencies and amplitudes place them in the area of surviving hearing. (Remember that weaker sounds are near the top, stronger sounds are near the bottom.)

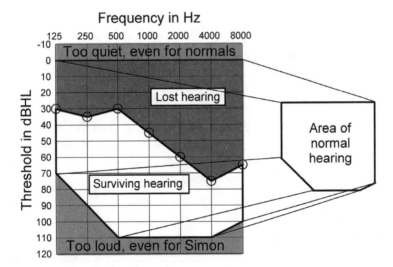

Figure 6–3. Pure-tone thresholds for Simon's right ear. The threshold line divides the area of normal hearing into two areas. Above the line is the area of "lost" hearing. Below it is the area of "surviving" hearing.

More About Discomfort

You will have noticed in Figure 6–3 that the area of surviving hearing in Simon's right ear is smaller than the area of normal hearing. Perhaps this seems a little odd. One might assume that the thresholds of hearing and discomfort would shift by the same amount, leaving the total area of hearing unchanged. To a certain extent this might be true for a conductive hearing loss, but Simon's impairment is sensorineural. Recall from Chapter 5 that a characteristic of a sensorineural impairment is a rapid growth of loudness with increasing amplitude, a phenomenon known as *loudness recruitment*. Simon cannot hear weak sounds, but strong sounds are loud. And sounds that are too loud for comfort in the normal ear may be just as loud and uncomfortable for Simon, hence the reduced area between the thresholds of hearing and discomfort.

Speech and the Audiogram

Our main concern with Simon's hearing loss is its impact on spoken language development. This is determined, in part, by his ability to hear the speech around him. Figure 6–4 shows the audiogram for Simon's right ear together with the area covered by the sounds of typical speech at conversational distance (taken from Figure 2–3). Only about one third of this area falls within the area of surviving hearing. To make matters worse, the most important part of the speech signal, lying between about 1000 and 3500 Hz, is mostly in the area of lost hearing. In other words, if nothing is done to improve things, Simon will hear very little of the speech going on around him, even when directed at him. He will know when someone is talking but many of the important details will be missing. As a result, Simon's own development of spoken language will be delayed and defective. Note that Simon's three-frequency average hearing loss is 45 dB (average of thresholds at 500, 1000, and 2000 Hz).

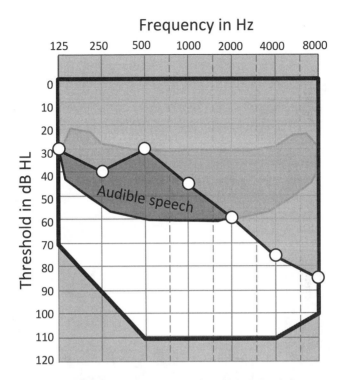

Figure 6–4. The audiogram for Simon's right ear shown in relation to the sounds of speech at conversational distance.

This places the loss in the "moderate" category (see Chapter 5) but the word "moderate" seriously understates the developmental consequences of this hearing loss, without appropriate intervention.

Speech for Different Degrees of Hearing Loss

The impact of various degrees of hearing loss on the audibility of speech is illustrated in Figure 6–5. Remember that this information relates to unassisted hearing (no aid, no implant) and the audibility of typical speech (not too soft, not too loud) at conversational distance (a few feet). Audiograms are shown for five degrees of sensorineural hearing loss.

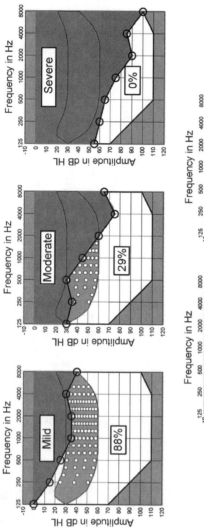

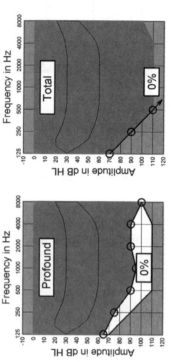

Figure 6–5. Typical audiograms for ears with different degrees of hearing loss showing their effects on the audibility of unamplified conversational speech. The numbers indicate the percentage of useful information that is available in the spectrum of conversational speech, using the "count the dots" approach of Chapter 2.

In Figure 6–5 we have estimated the percentage of audible speech information using the count-the-dots approach from Chapter 2. You will see:

a. A child with a *mild* hearing loss can detect most of the spectrum of conversational speech. Spoken language will develop spontaneously but difficulty in hearing soft and distant speech may slow vocabulary acquisition and could pose an educational risk.

b. A child with a *moderate* hearing loss can detect part of the spectrum of conversational speech. Spoken language will develop spontaneously but, because a lot of the important information is missing, there will be delays and deficits. With hearing aids, good audibility of conversational speech can be provided and, with appropriate management, the child should function as if he has a mild hearing loss.

c. A child with a *severe* hearing loss cannot detect the spectrum of conversational speech. He may, however, detect some of the spectrum of loud or close speech, including his own. Spoken language is unlikely to develop spontaneously. There is, however, a considerable area of surviving hearing and hearing aids can place most of the spectrum of conversational speech in this area. Unfortunately, there will be a loss of clarity because of the sensorineural damage, but, with appropriate management, one can expect good spoken language development.

d. A child with a *profound* hearing loss cannot detect speech even when loud and nearby. He does not hear his own speech efforts. Spoken language will not develop spontaneously. High-powered hearing aids can render speech partially detectable, but the tiny area of surviving hearing, combined with a serious loss of clarity, limit their benefit. With intense auditory-oral intervention, spoken language can develop but with delays and deficits. Cochlear implants, however, can provide these children with more and better hearing than they will experience with hearing aids

e. In extreme cases, the hearing loss can be *total*. The result is a "bottom left hand corner audiogram" produced because the child feels the vibrations of low-frequency sound. There is no area of surviving hearing into which a hearing aid can place the speech spectrum. Although it is not impossible for a child to develop spoken language in the absence of hearing, the results are seldom good. Moreover, there are very few teachers with the specialized skills needed to work successfully with such children in an oral setting. Fortunately, the cochlear implant can often provide a totally deaf child with hearing that is equivalent, in sensitivity and clarity, to that of a child with a moderate or severe loss who is fitted with hearing aids.

Measuring Threshold

One might wonder how one can obtain pure-tone audiograms from very young children. In other words, how can we determine the lowest amplitude at which a pure tone stimulus produces a sound sensation? In fact, audiologists have several tools at their disposal. One possibility is to examine the auditory brainstem response (ABR) to tones of varying amplitude. The ABR consists of electrical activity in the brain that can be recorded from electrodes placed on the scalp (see Figure 6–6a). This test can be done while a child is sleeping and is used both for screening the hearing of newborns and for more complete evaluation. The technique can be used at any age, though cooperation may be difficult with toddlers.

The other alternative is behavioral testing. Starting around 6 months of age, children can be conditioned to turn to look at an animated toy or video display when they hear a tone (Conditioned Orientation Reflex or COR testing [Figure 6–6b]). This procedure remains viable up to around 18 months of age, after which children tend to lose interest quickly. From around three years of age, one can use Play Audiometry, in which the child is taught to respond with some activity such as placing a ring on a tower, or putting a

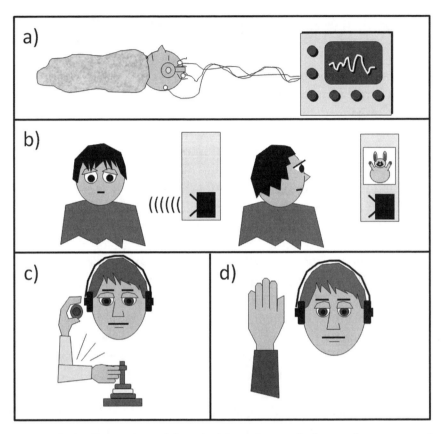

Figure 6–6. Examples of threshold testing techniques that are used with children: (a) Auditory Brain-stem Response (ABR) testing in which electrical activity of the brain is detected in response to sound; (b) Conditioned Orientation Reflex (COR) testing in which the child learns to associate sound with an interesting event and turns to look in anticipation; (c) Play audiometry in which the child is taught to delay a play activity until he hears a sound; and (d) For older children, a simple act such as hand raising to confirm that a sound was heard.

block in a bucket (Figure 6–6c). By around 5 years of age, children can usually be instructed to raise their hand when they hear a tone (Figure 6–6d).

Other Hearing Tests

The air-conduction pure-tone audiogram provides only basic information on hearing sensitivity. You have seen how this information can be enhanced by the addition of bone-conduction testing, to reveal the presence and magnitude of any conductive impairment. You have also seen how examination of the audiogram in relation to the area of normal hearing and the speech banana can provide insights into the developmental implications of the loss (assuming no intervention). We can also estimate the area of surviving hearing that is available for speech that is amplified by hearing aids. But a full assessment of hearing involves much more than this.

Acoustic immittance testing involves the application of known amounts of sound energy into the ear canal and measurement of the resulting sound level. The way this level varies as pressure on the ear-drum membrane is changed provides considerable information on the condition of the middle ear and can help determine what is wrong. The process is known as *tympanometry* and the result is a tympanogram. Another use of immittance testing is to detect the contraction of a muscle in the middle ear in response to strong sound. This tells us something about the perception of loudness and the condition of some of the nerve pathways involved in hearing.

Recent decades have seen the development of techniques for direct examination of the function of the cochlea. These tests involve the detection of *otoacoustic emissions* (OAEs) which are very weak sounds generated by the cochlea as it responds to a sound stimulus. The results do not provide an audiogram but they can be used for the diagnosis of auditory neuropathy and other conditions in which messages from the cochlea are not properly transmitted to the brain.

Speech perception testing is used with adults and older children as an indirect method of assessing the clarity of sound sensations once they are loud enough to be heard. With very young children who have yet to develop spoken language skills, we can assess their ability to detect the acoustic contrasts that signal differences among phoneme classes (see Chapter 2). The methods are similar to those used in assessing threshold but the child is conditioned to respond to a change in an ongoing string of repeated syllables. At some time in the future it may be possible to assess clarity from electrophysiologic (brain wave) responses to a phonemic change but this approach is, at the time of writing, still being researched. Once the child reaches 3 years of age it usually is feasible to use tests of syllable or word repetition to assess hearing clarity. If there is concern that results are being limited by immature speech skills, one can use identification tasks involving a limited set of toys or pictures, carefully chosen to emphasize specific phonetic contrasts (e.g., "Show me the pea," "Where is the bee?"). At the time of writing, and in spite of several years of research on this topic, the techniques just described for measuring the clarity of sound sensations are not widely used in the audiologic evaluation of very young children. The most common approach is to make inferences about sound clarity from the ongoing development of listening, speech, and language skills. Unfortunately, this information comes after the fact and cannot be used for initial planning of a program of intervention. It can, however, be useful for tracking progress and, perhaps for suggesting changes in intervention strategy.

Back to Simon

What have we learned from Simon's audiogram in Figure 6–1? First, the absence of a gap between air-conduction and bone-conduction thresholds told us that the impairment is entirely sensorineural. If we wanted further confirmation we could perform immittance testing. If we wanted more information about the nature of the sensorineural impairment, we could perform oto-acoustic emissions testing and/or acoustic reflex testing. We also see that around two thirds of the conversational speech banana falls into Simon's area of lost hearing. To make matters worse, the most important region, between 1000 and 3500 Hz is inaudible. This tells us that, without intervention, there will be major delays and deficits of spoken language development with serious consequences for cognitive, intellectual, and social-emotional development (see Chapter 4). Because Simon can detect the lower frequencies of conversational speech, it would have been difficult for his parents to realize that he had serious hearing difficulties. This could account for the fact that he was already 18 months old before receiving a full audiological evaluation. On the positive side, we can see that Simon has a substantial area of surviving hearing into which we can place the conversational speech spectrum when it is amplified (made louder) by a hearing aid (see Chapter 7).

The results of many years of experience tell us that, even with this amount of sensorineural damage, the chances are that the clarity of the amplified speech will be fairly good. If we wanted more information on this point, we could assess Simon's ability to hear differences among speech sounds, after they have been amplified by hearing aids. But such tests would be of limited value until Simon has had several months of listening experience.

It is critical that the Simon's parents understand that hearing aids do not restore normal hearing. They may also need to be coached in ways to enhance his experience of sound and language to make up both for the imperfections of aided hearing and the time that has been lost.

Some Things to Remember

1. Basic hearing testing involves measuring the **thresholds** for detection of pure-tones of various frequencies.

2. Supplementing **air-conduction** testing with **bone-conduction** testing helps distinguish sensorineural from conductive hearing loss.

3. The line joining thresholds on an audiogram separates the area of normal hearing into areas of **lost** and **surviving** hearing.

4. Adding the speech "banana" to the audiogram form shows the effect of degree of loss on the **audibility** of conversational speech.

5. The resulting information provides insights into the **developmental consequences** of the hearing loss (without intervention).

6. The area of surviving hearing also indicates the potential benefit of amplification with **hearing aids**.

7. Hearing threshold can be measured in young children using both **electrophysiological** (brain wave) and **behavioral** techniques.

8. **Other tests** provide more detailed information on the function of the middle ear, the function of the cochlea, and the clarity of sound sensations.

Relevance

The ability to read and interpret audiograms and other hearing test results can be a great asset to teachers, clinicians, and parents. It can play a role in understanding a child's strengths and weaknesses, intervention planning, outcome assessment, and parent counseling.

To Learn More

■ Chapters 4 through 10 of *Pediatric Audiology*, edited by Jane Madell and Carol Flexer, provide a thorough review of techniques used for newborn hearing screening and for full audiological evaluation (Madel & Flexer, 2008).

■ For another thorough treatment of pediatric hearing testing, we suggest Chapter 4 of the *Comprehensive Handbook of Pediatric Audiology* by Seewald and Tharpe (2010).

CHAPTER 7

Hearing Aids and Cochlear Implants

Overview

In earlier chapters, we stressed the key role of hearing in a child's acquisition of spoken language. It follows that a first step in the management of childhood hearing loss should be to provide hearing assistance and to make assisted hearing as good as it can be. There are two viable options; hearing aids and cochlear implants. Hearing aids make sound louder. If there is enough surviving hearing, they provide audibility of sounds that, otherwise, are too weak to be heard. Unfortunately for children with sensorineural hearing loss, the sound from the hearing aid must still be fed to a defective cochlea. If the deficits are not too great, as in mild, moderate, or moderately severe hearing loss, hearing aids can be highly effective but, for children with very severe, profound, or total sensorineural loss, hearing aids are of limited benefit. Cochlear implants, however, stimulate the auditory nerve with electrical signals derived from the sound stimulus. Because they bypass the defective cochlea, implants usually provide better assisted hearing than hearing aids for children with very severe, profound, or total hearing loss. Neither hearing aids nor cochlear implants provide assisted hearing that is as good as normal hearing but, for many children with sensorineural hearing loss, assisted hearing is good enough to play its natural role in the acquisition of spoken language providing other aspects of management allow for its shortcomings.

Goals

Auditory-oral intervention begins with hearing assistance, the goal of which is to make hearing capacity is as good as it can be. To accomplish this, we need to satisfy four criteria:

1. **Audibility.** Quiet but significant sound stimuli should generate sound sensations. We particularly want the child to detect the most important sounds of speech, even when spoken at a distance.

2. **Comfort.** Loud sounds should not cause discomfort or risk further hearing damage.

3. **Resolution.** Different sound stimuli should generate different sound sensations. In other words, the child should be able to distinguish among sounds that differ in terms of frequency, spectrum, amplitude, and pattern of change over time. We particularly want the child to be able to hear differences among the sound patterns of speech.

4. **Consistency.** There should be a consistent and predictable relationship between sound stimulus patterns and the resulting patterns of sound sensation. The child's developing brain needs to know that assisted hearing is a reliable source of information about events in the environment.

When these four components of hearing *capacity* are present, the child has the opportunity to develop the basic hearing *skills* of:

a. Awareness and alerting (hearing sounds),

b. Listening (sustaining attention to sound patterns),

c. Discrimination (awareness of differences among sounds),

d. Recognition (identifying sounds and the events that caused them), and

e. Localization (determining the direction a sound comes from).

The first four aspects of skill are attainable with good auditory capacity in only one ear. The fifth requires good capacity in both ears. At the time of writing there are two options for enhancing hearing capacity: hearing aids and cochlear implants.

The Hearing Aid

The hearing aid makes the sound stimulus stronger and the sound sensation louder—a process we call amplification. The amount by which the sound stimulus is amplified is referred to as the gain of the hearing aid. Imagine an aid with a gain of 30 dB. If we put sound with an amplitude of 60 dB SPL into the microphone (the input), then the sound that comes out of the hearing aid (the output) will have an amplitude of 90 dB SPL. In other words:

Input + Gain = Output

As you might have guessed, things are not quite that simple:

a. *Gain curve.* The child will need different amounts of gain at different frequencies. Any hearing aid also has low and high frequency limits beyond which it cannot provide effective gain. The relationship between gain and frequency is known as the "gain curve" or "frequency response" of the aid.

b. *Amplitude compression.* The child will need different amounts of gain for different input amplitudes. For example, loud sounds don't need as much amplification as quiet sounds. The process of reducing gain as input increases (and increasing gain when amplitude falls) is known as amplitude compression. It compresses a wide range of input amplitudes into the child's reduced area of surviving hearing.

c. *Output limiting.* There is a limit to the highest sound amplitude the aid can generate. This limit must be selected or adjusted to satisfy the comfort and safety needs of the individual child.

Earmolds

At the time of writing, most pediatric hearing aid fittings are of behind-the-ear aids. These usually require a tube to feed amplified sound into the child's ear canal. The *earmold* is used both to hold the tube in place and to control the amount of sound that is allowed to leak out of the ear canal. This little piece of plastic can have a big influence on the performance of the hearing aid. If it does not fit accurately, or if it comes loose, the gain and output are reduced, especially in the low frequencies. In addition, the hearing aid may start whistling because of excessive *acoustic feedback* (the leakage of sound from the ear canal back to the microphone). Because they are still growing, young children need frequent earmold replacement to maintain the best possible assisted hearing.

If the hearing loss is confined to the higher frequencies, the audiologist may deliberately provide a controlled leak in the form of a *vent* (that is, a hole in the earmold that allows some of the low frequency sounds to escape from the ear canal). The vent also allows natural low frequencies into the ear canal. As you might imagine, the vent also increases the likelihood of whistling. Modern digital hearing aids, however, provide the option of feedback control to reduce the likelihood of whistling.

Hearing Aid Fitting

The selection and adjustment of hearing aids is the responsibility of the pediatric audiologist, whose initial decisions are based on three sorts of information:

1. The best estimate of the child's pure-tone thresholds.

2. Published data on typical discomfort levels.

3. *Either* published data on the typical acoustic characteristics of children's ears at various ages, *or* direct measures of the

acoustic characteristics of the child's ear (to determine what is known as the real-ear-to-coupler difference or RECD).

From this information, the audiologist generates target characteristics, using computer programs designed to provide audibility of soft speech, while avoiding discomfort from loud speech. After adjusting the aid, the audiologist seeks to verify that the fitting targets have been met, using special test equipment. As you can imagine, the fitting and verification processes call for considerable knowledge and expertise on the part of the pediatric audiologist.

More About Real-Ear-to-Coupler Difference (RECD)

Hearing aid performance is usually measured by supplying the amplified sound to a sealed, hard cavity (known as a coupler), whose volume approximates that of the average adult male ear. It has long been recognized, however, that the sound generated in the ear of the user can be quite different, especially when the user is a small child. For this reason, the recommended practice for hearing aid fitting is to measure performance in the "real ear." This requires placement of the aid and earmold in the ear, together with a fine tube that carries the sound from the ear canal to a measuring microphone. As you can imagine, young children are unlikely to cooperate long enough for completion of all the measurements and readjustments required, especially as some of these involve generating fairly loud sounds. An ingenious solution to this problem, however, was developed by Richard Seewald and his colleagues at the University of Western Ontario. A standard signal containing all the frequencies of interest is first sent into the child's ear and then into the standard coupler. Measurements of the sound spectrum, with the earmold in place, are made in the ear and the coupler. The difference is the RECD. The beauty of this technique is that the child needs to cooperate for only one brief measurement. After this, all measurements and adjustments are carried out in the standard coupler, using the RECD as a correction factor.

More About Hearing Aids

For many years, hearing aids had just four main components:

1. A *microphone* to convert sound patterns into electrical patterns.

2. An *amplifier* to increase the size of the electrical patterns.

3. A *receiver* (a tiny loudspeaker) to convert the electrical patterns back into sound.

4. A *battery* to provide the extra energy and make the amplifier work.

Additional features could have included a volume control, a tone control, an adjustment of maximum output, and directional microphones that picked up sound a little better from in front than from behind. These aids were referred to as analog aids because the electrical patterns in the aids were analogous to the sound patterns (see the upper panel of Figure 7–1). With the advent of digital technology, a new component has been added: a tiny computer. The electrical patterns generated by the microphone are changed into strings of numbers. These numbers are manipulated (processed) before being changed back into electrical patterns for conversion to sound (see the lower panel of Figure 7–1). Although we refer to these as digital hearing aids, they are actually analog aids with a computer added. The computer and its associated software allow a much greater range of control. For example, the signal can be split into several frequency bands with independent adjustment of amplification characteristics. Additional possibilities include enhanced directionality, processing to render background noise less intrusive, and acoustic feedback suppression to avoid the annoying whistle that hearing aids are prone to.

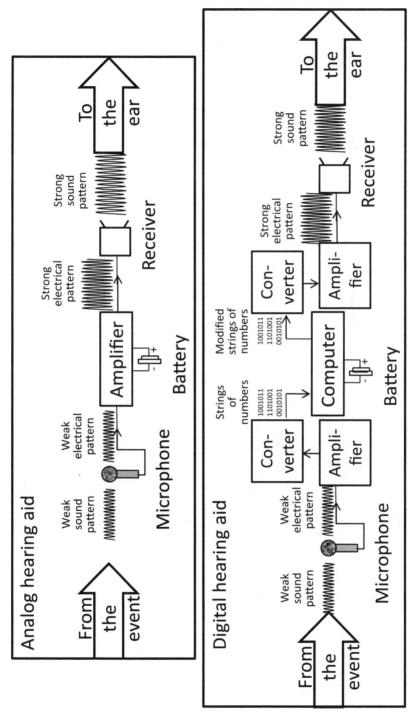

Figure 7-1. The main components of a hearing aid.

Showing Aided Thresholds

Once a hearing aid is in place, it is possible to repeat pure-tone threshold testing using loudspeaker presentation. The result is an aided audiogram that shows the weakest sound the child can now detect at several frequencies. Figure 7–2 shows such an audiogram for the right ear of Simon, whom we introduced in Chapter 6. Using the count-the-dots approach, in the left panel, we see that the aid has increased audibility of the information in the typical conversational speech spectrum from 29% to 88%. Using the phoneme distribution approach, in the right panel, we see that Simon has gained access to several otherwise inaudible speech sounds. Unfortunately, he still has difficulty detecting some high-frequency stops and fricatives —especially the sounds "s," "t," and "k."

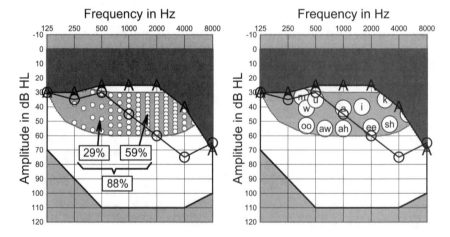

Figure 7–2. Simon's aided and unaided thresholds (right ear only) in relation to the speech spectrum. The left panel shows how the hearing aid increases speech audibility from 29% to 88%, based on counting dots. The right panel shows improvement in audibility of some, but not all, speech sounds.

Showing the Amplified Speech Spectrum

The aided audiogram is convenient but it does have a serious limitation. By showing the *aided* threshold in relation to the *unamplified* speech spectrum without adjusting the threshold of discomfort, we create the false impression that the aid has increased the area of surviving hearing. An alternative approach is to show the child's *unaided* audiogram in relation to the *amplified* speech spectrum, as illustrated in Figure 7–3. When we examine the situation in this way, we are showing the effect of the hearing aid on the sound presented to the listener rather than what happens to the listener's threshold when he is wearing the hearing aid. In Simon's case, we can see that, in spite of the reduced area of surviving hearing, there is room to spare. He will maintain audibility of the speech signal even if its amplitude rises or falls.

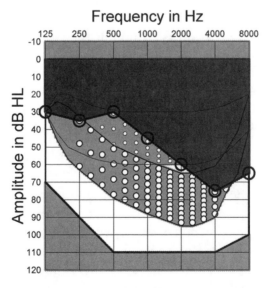

Figure 7–3. The amplified and unamplified speech banana in relation to Simon's right ear threshold.

The benefit of showing amplified speech in relation to the unaided threshold is illustrated in Figure 7–4. The amplified speech banana fits comfortably into the area of surviving hearing for mild and moderate loss. It also fits fairly well for the severe loss, although there is little room for change in speech amplitude. For the profound loss, the restricted area of surviving hearing isn't big enough to accommodate all the information in the speech signal. And for the total loss there is, by definition, no surviving hearing.

Figure 7–4 illustrates one of the reasons why the potential benefit of hearing aids falls with increasing degree of hearing loss; the area of surviving hearing shrinks, eventually becoming too small to accommodate the area covered by the speech spectrum. This approach to illustration, however, does have a few limitations:

a. In this figure, some arbitrary assumptions were made about the frequency response and average gain of the hearing aid. Different assumptions could have increased some of the numbers. This is good news, although the overall pattern would not change.

b. This figure says nothing about the effects of changing the average amplitude of the speech entering the hearing aid. Speech at the ear (including that of the child's own speech) can be as much as 15 dB higher in amplitude than speech at conversational distance. This is good news.

c. The count-the-dots approach is based on data relating only to segmental speech patterns, that is, vowels and consonants. The lower frequencies, however, especially those around 500 Hz, also carry useful suprasegmental information (see Chapter 2) which is not accounted for here. This is good news.

d. With fast-acting amplitude compression, it is possible to reduce the amplitude differences between the weaker and stronger

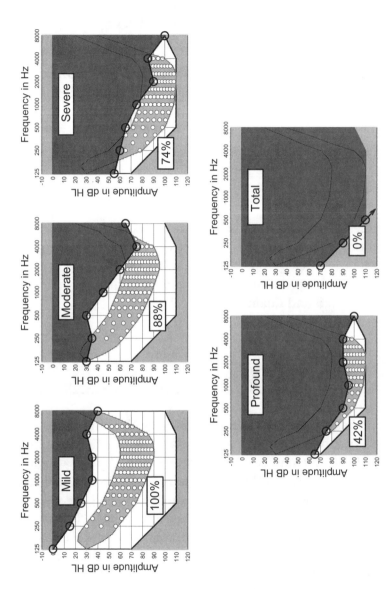

Figure 7–4. The amplified speech spectrum, for typical conversational speech, in relation to threshold for five degrees of hearing loss. The numbers show estimates of the percentage of speech information that is detectable via the hearing aid, based on counting dots.

sounds within a word. The result is compression of the speech banana in the vertical direction, possibly providing an increase in audibility for the severe and profound hearing loss. This is good news.

e. The count-the-dots approach, however, does not account for the loss of resolution (or clarity) that accompanies sensorineural hearing loss. The numbers in Figure 7–4 only tell us about audibility. They say nothing about resolution. If we were to account for the effects of reduced resolution all the numbers would be reduced. And the reduction would increase with hearing loss. This is bad news.

Regardless of potential adjustments to the details, the principal conclusion holds: hearing aid effectiveness tends to fall as degree of hearing loss increases, approaching zero as the loss approaches total. Numerous research studies and years of clinical experience have demonstrated and quantified this relationship.

Hearing Aids and Sound Resolution

Of the four basic goals of hearing assistance, hearing aids only address the first two. They can improve audibility while avoiding discomfort. Unfortunately, resolution is determined mainly by the integrity of the sensorineural system. There is nothing the aid can do to increase the resolution of a damaged ear. The best we can hope for is that the hearing aid allows the child to make full use of whatever resolution his auditory system is capable of. To this end we want hearing aids that introduce as little distortion as possible. We also want aids that provide good audibility of high frequencies —better than that shown in Simon's case.

More About Hearing Aids and Resolution

Loss of hair cells reduces the cochlea's ability to provide the brain with the information needed to differentiate sounds. It also makes it difficult for the child to separate sounds that occur at the same time. These problems are made worse by distortion in the hearing aid. One of the worst offenders is *intermodulation distortion*, which causes the generation of new sounds in the output that were not present in the input. These sounds provide no useful information and can interfere with what the child needs to hear. Manufacturers try to minimize this kind of distortion in hearing aids but it can develop over time. Measurement of distortion should be included in periodic hearing aid checks.

Hearing Aids and Consistency

The fourth requirement of hearing assistance is consistency. The child's developing brain needs a consistent relationship between the sound stimulus and the sound sensation. Too many adaptive features in the hearing aid can undermine consistency. Amplitude compression and output limiting are necessary for the young child with sensorineural hearing loss and feedback suppression can only be helpful. But some other features of modern digital hearing aids such as noise reduction and adaptive directionality may not be. Developments in hearing aid technology are driven mainly by the needs of the large market of adults with acquired hearing loss. It should not be assumed that the latest and greatest in digital signal processing is also best for the developing child.

More About Consistency

Two of the adaptive features of modern digital hearing aids are noise management and adaptive directionality. Both are aimed at improving speech understanding in noise—a task that most hearing aid users find challenging. *Noise management* seeks to reduce amplification in one or more frequency regions at times when the aid decides that the signal there is probably not speech. *Adaptive directionality* seeks to reduce amplification for nonfrontal sounds when the aid decides that the noise level is high, sometimes taking account of the direction the noise seems to come from. We believe both processes to be inappropriate for infants with hearing loss. Apart from the fact that they undermine the consistency on which the brain is relying, they actually work against the development of basic hearing skills. The child is just discovering what sound and hearing can tell her about the world, which is all around her, and which she is also discovering. Suppressing nonspeech sounds can only interfere with this process. And suppressing non-frontal sounds undermines the 360 degree benefit of hearing and its role as watchdog sense. Later on, when basic hearing skills are in place and spoken language has become a major feature of the child's life, such schemes may be beneficial under circumstances in which the primary concern is the speech of a talker at whom the child is looking.

Amplifying Nonspeech Sounds

Current practice in hearing aid fitting mainly addresses the need for comfortable audibility of speech. This has been the focus of our discussion so far. It is a reasonable approach, given that the most serious consequences of childhood hearing loss arise through delays and deficits in acquiring spoken language. For the child who is just discovering sound and hearing, however, and learning what they can tell her about the world, speech is only one of the events she is concerned with. There is a whole world of sound out there. Fortunately, hearing that has been optimized for the audibility of speech is also appropriate for audibility of most nonspeech sounds. It is true that pure tones with very low frequencies (below around 250 Hz) will be difficult to hear. Fortunately, however, very low-frequency sounds, such as the rumble of an approaching truck, are not pure tones but complex sounds that include pure-tone components at higher frequencies.

We already stressed the importance of good high-frequency hearing. Unfortunately, hearing aids are not very good at amplifying very high-frequency sounds such as the cheep of a newly hatched chicken. This problem results from the inability of tiny microphones and receivers to reproduce very high frequencies. At the time of writing, however, efforts are under way to improve the high-frequency performance of hearing aids, either by extending the range of amplification, or by artificially shifting high-frequency sounds to lower frequencies, a process known as *frequency transposition* or *frequency compression*. If successful, these developments could improve hearing for both speech and nonspeech sounds.

Cochlear Implants

As you saw in Figure 7–4, the limited area of surviving hearing in children with profound or total hearing loss makes it difficult or impossible for them to detect all of the information in the sound patterns of speech. To make matters worse, even the sounds they can detect are not heard clearly. There is, however, an alternative. In the past few decades, the multichannel cochlear implant has revolutionized hearing assistance for children with profound and total hearing loss. It is now possible to provide a totally deaf child with assisted hearing capacity that is equivalent to that of a child with a moderate or severe hearing loss using hearing aids. The implant does this by bypassing the conductive mechanism, and the damaged cochlea, to deliver information directly to the auditory nerve for transmission to the brain. The deliverers and translators of Figure 3–2 have been rendered redundant, as illustrated in Figure 7–5.

More About Cochlear Implants

At the time of writing, the multichannel cochlear implant has both external and internal components, as illustrated in Figure 7–6.

Externally, there is:

a. A microphone to convert sound patterns to electrical patterns,

b. A computer to convert the electrical patterns into numbers for analysis and processing, and

c. A transmitter, held in place by a magnet, to send the results across the skin.

Internally, there is:

a. A receiver to accept the signals from the transmitter, decode them, and send them to

b. A flexible array of electrodes, inserted into the cochlea under the cochlear partition.

The flow of electric current from one electrode to another stimulates nearby fibers in the auditory nerve, a function normally carried out by hair cells.

Note: The only thing the receiver in a cochlear implant has in common with the receiver inside a hearing aid is that it "receives" a signal. Otherwise, they are totally different devices.

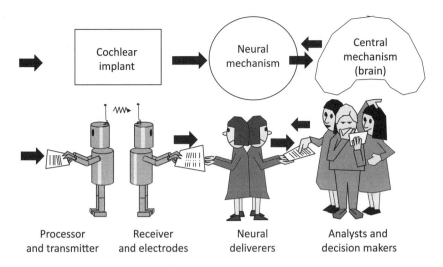

Processor and transmitter | Receiver and electrodes | Neural deliverers | Analysts and decision makers

Figure 7–5. Conceptual illustration of hearing with a cochlear implant.

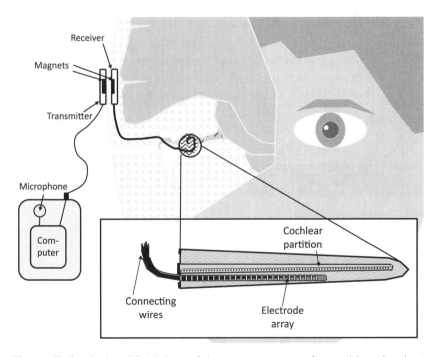

Figure 7–6. A simplified view of the components of a cochlear implant. The cochlea has been uncoiled to better illustrate the location of the electrode array. Note that the coiled shape of the cochlea prevents full insertion of this array. Note, also, that a very fine insulated wire connects each electrode to the receiver.

Cochlear Implant Mapping

The external processor of a cochlear implant has the task of analyzing the incoming sound and converting the results into patterns of electric current flow that are matched to the needs of the individual child. The process is analogous to the fitting of a hearing aid. Instead of an audiogram, however, the audiologist needs information on sensitivity and discomfort for electric current flow in each of the available stimulation channels. This fitting process is referred to as *mapping*. The audiologist seeks to map sound patterns onto the electrical characteristics of the child's implanted hearing. The processing schemes used for mapping have evolved over time and differ from manufacturer to manufacturer. The basic goal, however, is to generate patterns of stimulation in the auditory nerve that are similar to those generated by the hair cells of an intact cochlea. This is done by splitting the input signal into several frequency bands, extracting the amplitude fluctuations from each one, and sending this information in the form of pulses of electric current to specific places along the electrode array.

Cochlear Implants and Resolution

Assuming that the goals of audibility and comfort have been attained, the implanted child's ability to differentiate one frequency from another is limited by the number of channels of stimulation. Under the best of circumstances, the number probably lies somewhere between 16 and 20. This is small when compared with the number of hair cells in the undamaged cochlea. It turns out, however, that as few as eight channels of stimulation can provide experienced listeners with good speech understanding in quiet. Unfortunately, the quality of implanted hearing can differ from child to child, depending on the availability of auditory nerve fibers close to the electrode array. A shortage of nerve fibers and too great a distance between them and the electrodes means fewer channels available to the child. Note, also, that frequency resolution is not the only issue. There is a limit to the speed with which the processor can update information to each electrode. The resulting limit of time resolution can affect the listener's ability to recognize both speech and non-speech sounds. The combination of reduced spectral resolution and reduced time resolution also affects the child's ability to separate one sound pattern from another.

Because of the limited resolution, the best implanted hearing is not as good as normal hearing. This is bad news. To make matters worse some children do not experience the best implanted hearing. This is also bad news. But, the young child's brain and nervous system are highly adaptable and, with experience, will learn to extract as much information as possible from the sound sensations generated by the implant, perhaps even learning to use information that we, as adults, ignore. This is good news.

Cochlear Implants and Consistency

Concerns over the developing brain's need for consistency apply to implanted hearing just as they do to amplified hearing. The use of features such as noise management or directionality should probably be avoided until the child has developed basic hearing skills and, even then, reserved for situations in which the child is trying to understand speech from a person at whom he is looking. As with hearing aids, however, amplitude compression, in which gain falls as input amplitude rises, is appropriate. Indeed, with cochlear implants, it is an integral part of the mapping process. As the child's cochlea adapts to the presence of the electrode array, there may be changes in its electrical characteristics that require readjustment of the map. Otherwise, frequent changes to the map should be avoided. They deprive the child's brain of the consistency it needs.

Hearing Aids Versus Cochlear Implants

When is a hearing aid the best choice for hearing assistance and when is a cochlear implant likely to be more effective? For the child with a total hearing loss, a hearing aid has little to offer, but there is a good chance of highly effective implanted hearing. For the child with a profound hearing loss, the implant can almost certainly provide better audibility than a hearing aid, and there is every chance that resolution will also be better. For the child with mild, moderate, or moderately severe hearing loss, both aids and implants can provide audibility but resolution will most likely be better with a hearing aid. For the child with a severe hearing loss, it is impossible to predict which will be the most effective from the audiogram alone. Note, however, that degree of hearing loss is by no means the sole criterion for decisions about cochlear implantation. Many other factors must be considered as parents deal with this difficult decision.

One or Two Implants

Another decision to be faced is whether to implant one ear or both. At the time of writing, the movement is toward the latter. And there is ample evidence to show that hearing with two ears is better than hearing with one. In some cases, the best option is an implant in one ear and a hearing aid in the other. Each provides the brain with a different kind of information and the two can be combined to improve sound recognition.

Whatever the choice, parents, teachers, clinicians, and educational administrators must not be misled into believing that either the hearing aid or the cochlear implant completely eliminate all hearing deficits. Hearing assistance is intended to provide the child with the best possible hearing capacity. But, at the time of writing, the best falls short of normal hearing.

Wireless Microphones (FM Systems)

There are three main enemies of clear hearing: distance, noise, and reverberation. As indicated in Chapter 1, sound amplitude falls with increasing distance from the source. Audibility then falls as the weaker sounds in the speech spectrum sink below threshold, or below the level of interfering noise. Obviously, the greater the noise, the more it interferes with speech audibility. *Reverberation*, which is the persistence of sound in a room because of repeated reflections, reduces time resolution. We are all affected by these factors, but individuals with hearing loss, whether using hearing aids or cochlear implants, are particularly susceptible. Wireless microphones offer a highly effective solution to this problem. By picking up the speech signal a few inches from the talker's mouth and transmitting it (usually via FM radio waves) to a wireless receiver connected to (or built into) the hearing aid or implant, all three effects are eliminated—just as if the talker were speaking directly into the aid or implant microphone. This technology has a long history in the entertainment industry and in classrooms for children with hearing loss. Knowing of its demonstrated benefits, there is a temptation to include it in the hearing assistance provided to young children with hearing loss. As with noise management and directionality, we would caution against its indiscriminate use. The child who is developing basic hearing skills needs to be hearing what is happening around him, especially sounds of his own making.

There are, however, some situations in which the benefits of using an FM microphone could outweigh the drawbacks. One could argue, for example, for the benefits of improved exposure to mother's speech when the child is lying awake in the crib and not attending to anything else. Later on, there will be circumstances in which the child needs to hear a specific talker at a distance. One example might be on a car trip, when the child is sitting in the back seat and the driver needs to maintain spoken contact. Another could be when the child is on the playground but being supervised at a distance (see Appendix C).

Some Things to Remember

1. The goal of hearing assistance is to provide the **best possible hearing capacity**.

2. Hearing capacity involves **audibility, comfort, resolution, and consistency**.

3. **Hearing aids** make sound louder and change its characteristics. The resulting sound patterns are delivered to the cochlea where surviving hair cells stimulate the auditory nerve

4. The sounds entering and leaving the hearing aid are known, respectively, as **input** and **output**. The difference between the two is the **gain** of the aid.

5. The gain of an aid **varies with frequency**.

6. The gain of an aid also varies with input amplitude to provide **amplitude compression**.

7. Properly fit hearing aids provide **audibility of speech while avoiding discomfort**.

8. Good aided speech audibility can be expected for children with **mild, moderate, and severe** loss.

9. Limited aided speech audibility can be expected in cases of **profound** loss and none if the loss is **total**.

10. **Aided resolution** depends on the integrity of the cochlea, which falls with increasing loss.

11. Cochlear implants **stimulate the auditory nerve** with patterns of electric current derived from sound. They have revolutionized hearing assistance for children with profound and total hearing loss by providing hearing that is often equivalent to that of a child with severe, or even moderate, hearing loss who wears hearing aids.

12. The **decision to implant** is based on many considerations, of which degree of hearing loss is only one.

13. **Implanted resolution** depends, not only on the number of electrodes, but also on their distance from the surviving fibers of the auditory nerve, and on the speed with which the processor can update the information sent to the electrodes.

14. **Fitting** of hearing aids and **mapping** of cochlear implants involve adjustment to the needs of the individual child. Both require high levels of expertise on the part of the pediatric audiologist.

15. **Distance, noise, and reverberation** are the three main enemies of clear hearing. They can be counteracted with an FM system, but only for the speech of the person with the wireless microphone.

16. The developing brain's need for consistency suggests **caution** in the use of noise management, directionality, and wireless microphones, especially with the child who is developing basic hearing skills. The same caution applies to making frequent changes to the characteristics of an aid or the map of an implant.

17. The most important thing to remember is that **hearing aids and cochlear implants do not provide normal hearing**. If they did, there would be no need for the rest of this book.

To Learn More

- *Understanding Hearing Aids* by Taylor and Mueller (2011) provides detailed information on hearing aids at an introductory level.

- For a comprehensive text on pediatric cochlear implants, we suggest *Clinical Management of Children with Cochlear Implants*, edited by Laurie Eisenberg (2009).

■ Chapter 3 of Eisenberg's text, by Roush and Seewald (2009) provides specific information on hearing aids for children.

■ More information on the effects of distance, noise, and reverberation can be found in *Sound-field Amplification* by Crandell, Smaldino, and Flexer (2005).

PART 2

Management of Hearing Loss in Young Children

In this part of the text, we deal with management of hearing loss in young children. Other terms that might be used for this work are Pediatric Aural Rehabilitation, and Auditory-Oral Intervention.

There are several goals. The first is to provide hearing assistance and to ensure that the resulting hearing capacity is as good as it can be. This is the topic of Chapter 8. But the child must learn how to use his assisted hearing. The development of hearing skill provides the topic of Chapter 9. In Chapter 10 we come to the core of this work, that is, the development of spoken language and its cognitive base. Chapter 11 deals with social-emotional development. Without social skills and a healthy self image, the foundations of communication are undermined and the value of language diminished. Finally, in Chapter 12, we discuss families. The family creates the child's primary learning environment and is an integral part of it. Moreover, every professional involved in the management of the young child must interact with her parents. An understanding of the parent experience and role and the development of effective ways of interacting with parents is a critical requirement.

We caution the reader that the deconstruction of the child's learning into hearing, language, and social-emotional function is artificial. It is a convenience for exposition but, in reality, these components are inseparable. The whole is greater than the sum of its parts. In fact, the reader will find that the chapters in Part 2 often overlap. Some of the material in Part 2 also overlaps or recapitulates material from Part 1. This may help the reader whose main interest is in intervention and who chooses to begin with Part 2.

CHAPTER 8

Hearing Capacity

The first goal of auditory management is to ensure that hearing capacity is as good as it can be. We assume that a pediatric audiologist has already taken care of fitting/mapping hearing aids and/or cochlear implants, as outlined in Chapter 7. We also assume that these devices provide the best match to the child's hearing characteristics—as well as it was possible to determine them. Ideally, this will have been done soon after the hearing loss was identified. Once the device has been fitted, however, parents, teachers, and clinicians have continuing roles to play in ensuring that the goal of "best hearing capacity" is met and maintained. Among other things, they need to ensure that the child's brain has consistent access to sound. This means full-time use of a device that is in perfect working order. It also means prompt identification and treatment of any changes in the child's hearing status. In addition, parents, clinicians, and teachers need to be sensitive to the negative effects of distance, noise, and reverberation and, wherever possible, eliminate them. Finally, they need to help the pediatric audiologist work toward the goal of best assisted hearing capacity by providing feedback on the child's emerging hearing skills.

Guiding Principles

In this and the following chapters, we begin with guiding principles. As we discuss the rationale behind them, we repeat some material from Chapters 1 through 7. We do this for the benefit of readers who are more interested in application and have turned directly to Part 2. Some of the principles are supported by research, others make sense from what we know about the underlying factors, and still others are based on clinical and classroom experience. We follow each principle with its implications for management. In the case of hearing capacity, we suggest four main principles:

1. The **early principle**—hearing assistance should be provided as early in life as possible

2. The **consistency principle**—the child's brain needs a consistent relationship between sound stimulus and sound sensation. Consistency has three components:

    a. Consistency of use—the device should be used during the child's waking hours.

    b. Consistency of the device—the device should be kept in full working order.

    c. Consistency of the child—hearing changes should be addressed promptly.

3. The **acoustics principle**—listening conditions should enable the best reception of important sounds.

4. The **feedback principle**—information on the child's emerging hearing skills should be fed back to the pediatric audiologist responsible for adjusting the device.

The Early Principle

Rationale

From what is known about sensory, cognitive, and linguistic development, it makes sense that the child with hearing loss should have the best hearing capacity as soon in life as possible. Early hearing assistance allows hearing skills to develop in synchrony with other aspects of development. Delay introduces developmental asynchrony, in which case knowledge and skills developed without hearing must be modified if the full benefits of assistance and intervention are to be realized. In other words, early hearing assistance, along with other aspects of early intervention, allows the child's learning to be developmental rather than remedial. The validity of these conclusions is supported by years of experience and, more recently, by the findings of research studies.

Hearing assistance cannot be provided, however, until the presence of a hearing loss has been confirmed and the type and degree have been determined. Until fairly recently, the typical age for provision of assistance was between 18 and 24 months. Three developments have reduced this delay:

1. Universal newborn screening has made it possible to identify and measure most hearing loss within the first few months of life.

2. Objective methods of assessment, using electrical responses in the brain, acoustic responses in the cochlea, and acoustic properties of the middle ear (see Chapter 6) have greatly improved our ability to generate the information needed for selection and adjustment of hearing aids and implants.

3. Devices, and the techniques needed for fitting them, have been adapted for use with very young children.

As a result of these developments, there is a good chance of hearing aids being fitted by 3 months of age, as recommended by the Joint Committee on Infant Hearing (JCIH) in their guidelines for Early Hearing Detection and Intervention (EHDI).

If test results point to the cochlear implant as the better form of assistance, and if this indication is supported by experience with hearing aids (and by other factors considered by professionals evaluating implant candidacy), then implantation can occur soon after the child's first birthday. Only in special circumstances does the Food and Drug Administration (FDA) currently support earlier implantation.

Even when hearing aids do not provide the best possible hearing capacity, it is not appropriate to ignore them while waiting for an implant. As just indicated, the child's progress with properly fitted hearing aids serves as one of the criteria for a decision to implant. Moreover, experience with amplified hearing, even if limited, can speed the child's later adjustment to implanted hearing. In addition, parents and child will have adjusted to the daily routines involved in wearing a device by the time the implant is provided.

There are, however, two cautionary notes. First, some children can pass the newborn screening test but develop a progressive hearing loss during the first weeks or months of life, delaying detection and assessment. Second, the precision with which we can measure type and degree of hearing loss in infants is not yet good enough to engender absolute confidence in our ability to find the best settings of hearing aids and cochlear implants. These factors work against the goal of providing the best hearing capacity at the earliest possible stage of development.

On the positive side, we should point out that "early" in this context is a relative term. There was a time when "early intervention" meant "by 4 years of age." Today, we aim for 3 months or less. Note, also, that failure to meet this guideline does not mean all is lost. Good perceptual, cognitive, linguistic, and social-emotional management can mitigate the effects of delayed assistance. Only if sensory assistance is delayed until the child is approaching the teenage years, can we say that the resulting hearing capacity is unlikely to have much influence on spoken language competence.

Implications

Of course, we can do nothing about early assistance retroactively. Parents and clinicians can, however, work to minimize delays during the assessment and fitting process. And, as indicated earlier, arriving at the desired goal may take time, during which parents, teachers, and clinicians play a key role by providing feedback to the audiologist.

The Consistency Principle

Rationale

The developing brain should be able to rely on assisted hearing as a consistent source of information about sound-making events. This is a principle that makes sense on the basis of current knowledge. The brain of the developing child must learn the relationships between sound sensations and the events that produced them. If the same event produces one sensation today and a different sensation tomorrow (or none at all tomorrow), it would follow that the brain's task is made more difficult. Time spent on figuring out how to deal with variations caused by inconsistency takes away from time spent on learning about the natural changes in the relationships between events and sensation; those caused, for example by changing distance or direction.

Implications

Consistency of Use

Many factors determine the consistency which the hearing aids or cochlear implants are worn. Ideally, the goal should be for the device to become part of the child. It should be put on at the start of the child's day and removed when she falls asleep.

Unfortunately, the ideal of full time use is not easily attained. Hearing aids on very young children are easily displaced. Many parents address this problem with headbands, caps, tape, or other approaches, as shown in Figure 8–1. A tether can also be helpful to prevent loss of the aid when it falls out.

The child may, of course, reject a hearing aid because of discomfort. This can become apparent because of fussing and crying or, in the older child, repeated removal. When this occurs, it is important to determine whether the discomfort is physical, manifested by soreness in or around the ear, or acoustic, manifested

Figure 8–1. Jamie's mother has found that a knitted cap is a good way to keep the hearing aid in place.

by negative responses to loud sounds. In either case, a visit to the audiologist is called for. If the discomfort is physical, it may be necessary to remake the earmold or adjust the connection between earmold and hearing aid. If the discomfort is acoustic, it will be necessary to adjust the characteristics of the hearing aid. Note, also, that there can be physical discomfort from the simple presence of an earmold in the ear. If the child accepts the earmold by itself, without the aid attached, or with the aid turned off, the problem is most likely acoustic and needs referral to the audiologist. If, however, he still rejects the aid, with no evidence of soreness, a graded approach to acceptance may be needed, with rewards for short periods of use, and interesting distractions.

Parents must be counseled about the need for full-time use but they should not be made to feel guilty if they fail to meet this goal. And, at all costs, they should avoid the hearing aid, or implant processor, becoming a source of conflict between them and their child. An important issue, here, is the parents' perception of the device. If it is seen as a painful reminder of the child's (and their own) imperfection, parents are likely to convey these negative feelings to the child whose reactions will reflect their own. In the worst case, parents' anger at the deafness becomes transferred to the device that was intended to improve hearing. At this point, the goal of full-time use of the device becomes intricately entwined with counseling as the parents work through the process of grieving for the perfect child they feel they have lost. Often, they must wait for the positive feedback that comes from the child's progress in hearing and speaking. And they must wait for their own acceptance of the device, and the hearing loss, as part of their child who, they will discover, is perfect after all.

Once again, all is not lost if the goal of full time use is not attained. The brain of the developing child is remarkably adaptive. Once it has acquired ways of knowing whether the device is in place or not, it will not be confused by the sudden absence of a sound as a component of experience. Indeed, an older child may choose to remove the device at certain times, to enjoy a period of relative silence. For the younger child, however, this kind of adaptation does add a layer of complication to development and is in danger of undermining the role of hearing as the "watchdog" sense. The message to parents should be "full-time use if possible, but do not feel bad if you fall short of this goal."

Consistency of the Device

There is no point in consistent use if the device itself is not maintained in full working order. Clinicians must instruct and coach parents in the development of a daily routine:

a. To check the status of batteries used to power the device.

b. To check for physical damage.

c. In the case of hearing aids, to use a hearing-aid stethoscope to listen for evidence of intermittent, distorted, scratchy, or weak output (Figure 8–2).

d. In the case of implants, to use whatever system the manufacturer provides to confirm that the processor is delivering the intended signal to the implanted receiver. Unfortunately, there is little the parents can do at this point to confirm that the implanted electrodes are delivering the intended electrical signals to the nerves of hearing. In any case, if the implant portion is considered part of the child, this step comes under consistency of the child.

e. In all cases, seek immediate repair or replacement in the event of malfunction. In the ideal situation, a properly adjusted backup should be available for use during repair.

We pointed out in Chapter 7 that the earmold contributes to the characteristics of the hearing aid. Unfortunately, the young child's ear is growing and the perfect earmold can become loose and leaky in just a few weeks. Replacement is then needed to maintain consistency. At that time a new Real Ear to Coupler Difference (RECD) should be obtained by the audiologist and the aid adjusted accordingly. New earmolds may be required every 2 or 3 months in the first 2 years of life and every 6 months between the ages of 2 and 4 years. It used to be that excessive whistling by the aid was a sign that the earmold needed replacement. The introduction of feedback suppression in digital hearing aids has removed this clue and increased the need for a scheduled plan of replacement.

Figure 8–2. When listening to a hearing aid, your own voice is the most available input. Speak at both low and high levels and be especially conscious of distortion when using the latter. It will take practice and experience to focus on the sounds of your own speech coming from the hearing aid while ignoring the sounds that bypass the hearing aid.

Consistency of the Child

Assisted hearing capacity is determined by a combination of the characteristics of the device and the characteristics of the child. The consequences of hearing fluctuation are likely to be the same as the consequences of device malfunction. Therefore, it is important to monitor the child's responses to assisted hearing.

Sometimes, a failure to respond in the expected manner can be the only clue to malfunction of the device. At other times it can be the child's hearing that has changed. Changes of hearing are particularly important for the user of a hearing aid because its output must pass through the conductive and sensorineural mechanisms. The change can be permanent, if caused by increased sensorineural impairment, or it can be temporary, if caused by a conductive impairment. (Temporary sensorineural change and permanent conductive change can occur but are not common.) For the implant user, permanent change may reflect a reduced ability of the implanted electrodes to deliver electrical current to the nerves of hearing. In all cases, the change threatens the goal of "consistent best hearing capacity" and it should be identified and acted on as soon as possible. This may involve audiologic evaluation, medical evaluation, or both, followed by prompt repair, if the device is at fault, or treatment, if the problem is a temporary shift in hearing. If an increase in hearing loss turns out to be permanent, the device or its adjustment will need to be changed accordingly.

By far the most common reason for a temporary change in a child's hearing is otitis media, that is, inflammation or infection of the middle ear (see Chapter 6). The early stages involve pressure reduction in the middle ear cavity resulting in reduced mobility of the ear drum. At this stage, the child may stop responding in the accustomed way but have no other symptoms. If the condition persists, however, an infection will quickly develop, the resulting pain and discomfort will be obvious, and the child should be seen by her pediatrician. Even in normally hearing children, recurrent, persistent ear infections undermine the consistency and reliability needed by the developing brain and can lead to long-term problems of auditory attention. For the child with a small area of hearing (see Chapter 6) who is using hearing aids, an ear infection can reduce hearing capacity to zero until the problem is resolved.

An ear infection will not affect the assisted hearing capacity for an implanted child, but there are other medical risks and prompt follow-up is equally important.

So how can parents and teachers monitor a child's assisted hearing? The key is the child's accustomed and expected responses to sound. If the child fails to respond in the way that parents, clinicians, or teachers have come to expect, this can be a sign of change in assisted hearing capacity. For the very young child, expected responses may be nothing more than quieting or cessation of sucking. At the very least, one should look for responses to low- mid- and high-frequency speech sounds—"oo," "ah," "sh," "s"—produced with normal effort. But don't overdo it. The child will quickly habituate (stop responding) to repeated sounds. Later, the child may be responsive to his own name. When he recognizes the name of objects, his responses in simple games ("where is your nose?" "show me your toes," etc.) can help confirm that there has been no change in assisted hearing. By far, the most reliable monitoring will come when the child is able to imitate sounds and words. At this point, imitation of all sounds of the Ling test (see below)—presented in random order—can be used to confirm not only detection, but also recognition, across a wide range of frequencies. When the child is first learning these more advanced activities involving response to speech, let him see your face, just as you would for a child with normal hearing. But, for occasional and informal monitoring of hearing, speak from one side of the child, or when she is not looking. We do not recommend covering your mouth. It is both unnatural and potentially confusing to the child.

The Ling Test

Several years ago, Daniel Ling suggested using five speech sounds for checking assisted hearing. The sounds were "oo," "ah," "ee," "sh," and "s." This resulted in what became known as the Ling five-sound test. Later, Ling added an extra low-frequency sound "m." When checking for detection, "oo," "ah," "sh," and "s" are enough. But if testing for recognition, using either multiple choice or imitation, there are benefits to using five or six sounds. In particular, one should look for the ability to distinguish "oo" from "ee," indicating sensitivity to information contained in the second vocal-tract formant (see Chapter 2).

The reader will have noticed that we just moved into the area of hearing skill. This is as it should be. The pursuit and maintenance of best hearing capacity underlies and serves the goal of best hearing skill, which is covered in the next chapter. As skills develop, their demonstration provides ongoing confirmation that hearing capacity is being maintained.

The Acoustics Principle

Rationale

According to an old English proverb: "There's many a slip twixt cup and lip." Similarly, much can happen to sound on its way from the event that produced it to the microphone of the hearing aid or implant. As we pointed out in Chapter 7, there are three enemies of perfect sound transmission: distance, noise, and reverberation. Their effects need to be kept in mind and, when possible, minimized.

Let's talk, first, about distance. The sound traveling directly from the event that produced it to the microphone that must receive it loses 6 dB of amplitude for every doubling of distance (see Chapter 1). This causes serious problems for assisted hearing. When speech is produced at a distance, or from another room, some of the weaker sounds fall below either the assisted threshold (which is always poorer than normal) or the level of interfering noise. Either way, they are no longer available to the child. An older child with advanced hearing skills may be able to use his knowledge to "fill in" the missing information (as can you) but the child who has yet to develop these skills cannot.

When the talker and the speaker are in the same room, the effect of distance on amplitude is somewhat offset by reinforcement from multiple reflections from walls, ceiling, and other surfaces (i.e., reverberation). These reflections are somewhat delayed, however, and if the delay is too long, the speech segments begin to smear into each other and clarity suffers. Reverberation effectively increases the child's hearing impairment by reducing resolution in the time domain (see Chapter 6).

It should be apparent from the foregoing that distance, noise, and reverberation are not independent factors. They interact with each other. For example, higher levels of noise and reverberation increase the negative effects of distance. Smaller distances reduce the negative effects of noise and reverberation. Parents, teachers, and clinicians do not need to become acoustic experts. They should, however, be aware of the effects of distance, noise, and reverberation, and of ways to minimize their negative effects.

Implications

To offset the effect of increased distance, you can raise your voice, just as you would for a child with normal hearing. At the same time you should seek to remove sources of unwanted noise.

When possible, keep distance to a minimum. Be aware, however, of the effect of reduced distance when speaking close to the microphone of the hearing aid or cochlear implant. Remember that the amplitude *increases* by 6 dB every time the distance is cut in half. The amplitude of speech produced at 3 inches (8 cm) from the child's microphone, for example, is over 24 dB higher than that of the same speech produced at a conversational distance of 4 feet (1.3 m). Modern devices are designed to reduce gain when the input is high, so as to keep sound within the child's area of hearing and avoid loudness discomfort. Nevertheless, this feature can distort the signal and you should avoid overtaxing aids and implants with unnecessarily loud, close speech. When holding a baby who is wearing a hearing aid or cochlear implant, do not raise your voice. Talk at an intimate level, just as you would to a child with normal hearing, and let the device do the "voice raising" for you. At this distance, there is no need to worry about the interfering effects of noise or reverberation. Your speech will be loud enough to overcome both.

We now turn to the issue of noise. In the present context, noise can be defined as any sound that interferes with what the listener needs to hear. If, for example, the baby is lying awake in his carrier and you are talking to him while going about some other activity, irrelevant sound sources such as a radio or TV must be considered interference noise, and should be turned off. If, on the other hand, the baby is lying awake in her crib and not listening to anything in particular, the speech from a radio or TV could well add to her experience of the sound patterns of spoken language. Other sounds, such as siblings playing in the next room or dishwashers running, may be considered noise when the child needs to hear your speech. But, at other times, these sounds are important parts of the soundscape for the developing child. She will learn, later, about the events that produce them. The idea is to shape the acoustic environment to provide full audibility of sounds the child needs to hear and to subdue those sounds that interfere with what she needs to hear.

The third factor is reverberation. A little reverberation can be a good thing when it increases the amplitude of speech in a room. But too much reverberation causes speech to interfere with itself. Living spaces are not usually too reverberant because carpets, curtains, and upholstered furniture tend to absorb sound rather than reflect it. Classrooms, however, often have many sound-reflecting surfaces and reverberation then needs to be reduced to the point where it does not interfere with the speech of teachers or other children. Professional help may be needed to evaluate the acoustic properties of preschool classrooms or day-care centers and to modify them when necessary.

We pointed out in Chapter 7 that one way to eliminate the negative effects of distance, noise, and reverberation is with a personal FM system. In such a system, a wireless microphone is linked to the hearing device in a one-way "walkie-talkie" arrangement (Figure 8–3). But FM systems should only be used when they meet a specific need. Usually, that need is to provide the child with clear access to the speech of a specific talker when that talker is at a distance, or is in an unavoidably noisy environment such as a

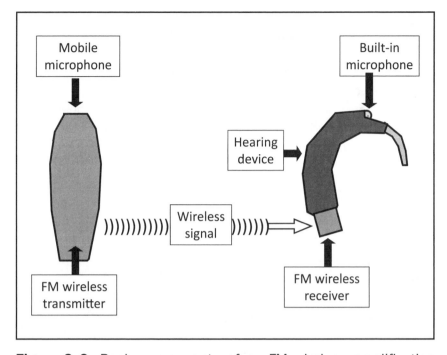

Figure 8–3. Basic components of an FM wireless amplification system. Note that the child using this system will have two microphones: one in his hearing device and a mobile one on the wireless transmitter.

car. But do not overdo it, especially with infants. The developing brain can be confused by indiscriminate use of a "roving ear" over which it has no control. As indicated earlier, the brain relies on a consistent and predictable relationship between event and sensation and this relationship is disturbed when an FM system is used. The caution about raising one's voice also applies to the use of an FM system. Talking into the wireless microphone is just like talking directly into the microphone of the hearing device. You must avoid the natural temptation to shout just because the intended listener is some distance away (a reaction often observed in telephone users).

A Bubble of Clear Hearing

One way of visualizing the effects of distance, noise, and reverberation on hearing is to imagine a bubble of clear hearing around the child, as illustrated in Figure 8–4. When speech is produced inside the bubble all the details are fully available. For the child with normal hearing in a quiet environment, that bubble is very large. If there is no noise or reverberation, a child with normal hearing can hear the weaker sounds in the speech of someone at a distance of 60 feet or more (around 18 meters). The introduction of noise reduces this distance (i.e., it shrinks the bubble) by an amount that depends on the amplitude of the noise. In heavy traffic, for example, the bubble is really small. The talker may need to be as close as 1 foot (30 cm) for full audibility. For the child wearing a hearing aid or cochlear implant, even in quiet surroundings, the bubble is already small. The weaker sounds of speech may become totally inaudible at a distance of only 20 feet (about 6 meters). Noise shrinks this bubble even further. Good acoustic management helps keep the bubble of clear hearing as large as possible. Note that an FM system does not enlarge the bubble. What it does is create a second bubble around the FM microphone.

The Feedback Principle

Rationale

There have been dramatic improvements in infant hearing assessment, pediatric hearing aid fitting, and pediatric implant mapping. In spite of this, the precision with which thresholds can be determined is not yet as high as the precision with which aids and implants can be adjusted. To make matters worse, our ability to measure resolution in infant hearing is rudimentary, and the infant

Figure 8–4. Ryan has a bubble of clear hearing whose size is determined by his assisted hearing thresholds and the background noise level. His teacher is in the bubble but his classmates are not. (Photograph courtesy of Clarke Schools for Hearing and Speech.)

cannot provide verbal feedback on sound quality or comfort. As a result, initial adjustments of hearing aids and implants inevitably involve educated guesses.

Implications

Much of the information needed by the pediatric audiologist as she refines the adjustments of aids and implants, and as she homes in on "best hearing capacity," must come from the people who observe the child in his everyday life, namely, parents, teachers, and clinicians. Channels of communication must be established and used to make this possible.

Some Things to Remember

1. A first step in management is to provide and maintain the best possible assisted **hearing capacity** on which other aspects of intervention will depend.

2. So that hearing skills can develop in synchrony with other aspects of development we seek to provide the best possible assisted hearing capacity as **early** in the child's life as possible.

3. We also seek to provide the developing brain with a **consistent** relationship between the events that produce sound and the resulting sound sensations experienced by the child.

4. To this end, we aim for full-time **use**; we monitor the **device** on a daily basis; and we seek prompt repair or replacement in the event of failure.

5. We also monitor the **child**'s responses to sound. If these change for the worse, we follow up promptly to determine whether the problem lies in the device or the child. If the latter, we seek prompt diagnosis and treatment.

6. In addition, we are conscious of the effects of **acoustics** and, if necessary, we control distance, noise, and reverberation so as to provide the developing child with optimum audibility of the sounds he needs to hear.

7. When these sounds are the speech of a single talker at a distance, or when the child is in very noisy surroundings, we may use an **FM system** to improve audibility, but we don't overdo it.

8. Finally, we monitor and observe the child's responses to sound and provide the pediatric audiologist with **feedback** to help her improve on the initial adjustments which were, inevitably, based on incomplete information.

To Learn More

■ Although they deal with early intervention in general, the studies of Yoshinaga-Itano, Sedey, Coulter, and Mehl (1988) and Moeller (2000), provide support for the conclusion that early sensory assistance increases the probability of successful outcome.

■ Information on the Joint Committee on Infant Hearing's (JCHI) recommendations can be found in their position statement (Joint Committee on Infant Hearing, 2007). This is also summarized at: http://www.asha.org/aud/articles/EHDI.htm .

■ A study by Spivak, Sokol, Auerbach, and Gershkovich (2009) showed that, among a group of around 200 early identified children in New York, only around 30% were fit with hearing aids by the target age of 6 months. These and similar data from other sources indicate that there is still work to be done in this area.

■ In December of 2010, the government reauthorized the Early Hearing Detection and Intervention (EHDI) act of 2000. This act provides support for States seeking to meet the recommendations of the Joint Committee on Infant Hearing. The original 2000 bill can be seen at: http://thomas.loc.gov/cgi-bin/query/z?c106:H.R.1193. The 2010 modifications can be seen at: http://www.thomas.gov/cgi-bin/query/D?c111:4:./temp/~c111kya6f5

■ Patricia Roush has provided a thorough review of the challenges encountered when fitting hearing aids on infants, highlighting the inevitable delay in arriving at the best possible hearing capacity (Roush, 2005).

■ There is a long history of research demonstrating the potential benefits of FM amplification in toddlers, school-aged children, and adults, all of whom have established listening skills and are unlikely to be confused by the "roving ear" effect. The relative benefits and costs for the infant who is still developing basic listening skills, however, have not been researched. The nearest example is a study that examined FM use in 2- to 4-year old children (Moeller, Donaghy, Beauchaine, Lewis, & Stelmachowicz, 1996).

CHAPTER 9

Hearing Skill

Overview

Hearing aids and cochlear implants enhance hearing capacity but if the child is to make use of this capacity she must develop hearing skill. In this chapter, we focus on nonspeech sounds. The goals are for the child to be alerted by important sounds, to listen, to pay attention to detail, and to interpret sounds in terms of both the events that produced them and their location. By far the most effective learning occurs when the child herself is responsible for making the sounds. Development of alerting and listening skills are further reinforced when adults with whom the child is interacting are aware of the soundscape themselves, demonstrate their own awareness of and interest in sounds, and take the time to show the child where and what they came from.

Guiding Principles

Once again we suggest certain guiding principles and their implications:

a. **The alerting principle**—the child needs to be alerted by potentially important sounds.

b. **The listening principle**—the child needs to pay attention to sounds; to listen.

c. **The discrimination principle**—the child needs to be aware of significant differences among sounds.

d. **The recognition principle**—the child needs to interpret sound in terms of the event that produced it, and to do so rapidly (see Chapter 3).

e. **The localization principle**—the child needs to be able to determine where the sound came from.

The Alerting Principle

Rationale

We have made several references to hearing as our watchdog sense. It alerts us to potentially important events in the environment such as voices, footsteps, car noises, or our name being called. Because hearing works at a distance, because sound travels around corners, and because our ears never close, hearing is ideally suited to this role. When hearing is imperfect, however, the developing brain is likely to ignore hearing and transfer the primary role of watchdog to vision and touch. Unfortunately, vision requires open eyes and line of sight and touch requires direct contact, strong structure-borne vibrations, or strong air movements. Both have their value for alerting but they are less effective than hearing. Once the child's brain has demoted hearing, it may be difficult to restore it to its dominant role even when hearing capacity has been optimized. One manifestation will be poor auditory attention. Normally hearing children with a history of frequent middle ear infections sometimes demonstrate persistent auditory attention difficulties that can affect language development and educational progress.

When first provided with a hearing aid or cochlear implant, the infant who has previously heard little or nothing will naturally be alerted by a change from silence to sound or by a sudden change of amplitude or spectrum. Evidence that the infant's attention has been captured can become apparent through cessation of activity, searching, startle, or, in some cases, crying. If the only significance is that "something happened," however, she may well habituate and stop responding. It is not that the sounds are no longer detected, but that they lack the power to take her attention away from other things. They lack salience. The adult's task is to give meaning to unexpected sounds; to provide salience.

Implications

What can we do to promote alerting? First, we need to become aware of the soundscape ourselves and to let the child see our own responses to potentially significant changes. Then we need to make her aware of the source. If necessary, we take her to see what made the sound and, if possible, we repeat the event that produced it. An example might be the squeak of a door or drawer when it opens, the onset of a rainstorm outside, the hammering of a worker in another room, a knock at the door, perhaps even the sound of a leaking faucet or a singing bird. We are talking here of sounds that are not central to the activity in which the adult and child were involved but sound that occurs unexpectedly. We draw the child's attention to the sound and we provide it with significance. We help the child learn that sound provides information about events that cannot be seen. At the same time, we are advancing the child's cognitive development and promoting sound recognition.

Adults can also take advantage of events that are known to be important to the child. The rattling of a spoon in a cup, for example, will already be associated with food and has a high probability of alerting the child to the imminence of feeding.

It is very important for both communication and safety that children be alerted when their names are called. Opportunities occur naturally during play and the activities of everyday living. Take as much advantage of them as you can. If the child does not respond at first, let her know that you were calling and demonstrate. The first time she responds spontaneously can be a memorable event for a parent.

A Memorable Event

A mother is chasing her implanted child around the house:

> Her eyes sparkled each time the chase resumed, her reddish hair wispy and loose, slipping out of her top knot. At one point, as I gained on her, sock skating down the burgundy stretch of dining room, I called out "I'm going to get you, Juliet!" and she turned her head to look at me.

> I stopped in my tracks like a roadrunner.

> "Juliet?" I ventured again. By now Juliet was smiling a huge smile—she had heard and recognized her name.

> "Juliet!" I choked and I scooped her into my arms. "I got you, Juliet. I got you."

From *If a Tree Falls* by Jennifer Rosner, Feminist Press, 2010. Used with permission.

The Listening Principle

Rationale

Listening requires sustained attention. Sometimes the attention is selective; the child listens to one sound while ignoring others. Here, however, we must acknowledge a basic problem. For children with sensorineural hearing loss, hearing aids and cochlear implants cannot provide normal sound resolution. In other words, the patterns of sound sensation lack some of the detail that would be available to a child with normal hearing. This problem can affect the development of listening skills in the same way that uncorrected defects of vision affect the development of seeing skills. The child with hearing loss must learn to listen with ears that are "out of focus," sometimes a little, sometimes a lot. Just how much detail is missing for an individual child will not be known in advance. Parents, teachers, and clinicians who are interacting with the child must be aware of this possible limitation and its effects on the development of all hearing skills, including listening. There is, however, a bright side. There is increasing evidence to suggest that listening experience can help the developing child's brain improve its ability to extract detail from the information provided by a damaged cochlea or a cochlear implant. This seems to be especially true for infants because the brain is still highly adaptable. In the case of cochlear implants, there is evidence to suggest that the infant's brain can learn to extract information from details in the patterns of electrical stimulation that would be unimportant for individuals with normal hearing. One should, therefore, pursue the development of listening skills in spite of early disappointments. In the interests of social-emotional development, however, these disappointments should be on the part of the adult, not the child.

Implications

Activities that promote alerting can lay the groundwork for listening. To encourage development of sustained attention to sound, however, we need to involve the child in activities that require him to identify and attend to sound sources. The goal is for the child to learn that sound is a valuable source of information, not just because of its presence, but because of its patterns. It also helps satisfy his pressing desire to learn about the world he finds himself in.

The Discrimination Principle

Rationale

As we are using the term here, discrimination goes beyond listening for details to distinguishing one pattern from another. Discrimination provides the foundation for recognition. Unfortunately, imperfections in assisted hearing capacity can limit the extent to which different sound stimuli produce different sound sensations. Such limitations will not become apparent, however, until the child has had the opportunity to learn and should not be assumed beforehand.

Implications

Discrimination ability should emerge during general listening activities. If specific attention to discrimination seems to be called for, it can involve games in which children use hearing to differentiate between toys that produce similar but different sound patterns. Such contrived activities are probably best restricted to the clinical or preschool environment, where they may be needed either to diagnose listening difficulties or to improve attention to details. For parents, we suggest the main focus should be on listening activities related to alerting, listening, and recognition.

The Recognition Principle

Rationale

Recognition depends, not just on listening skills, but also on cognition. As pointed out in Chapter 3, the child cannot recognize an object or event for which there is no place in his developing world model. The best he can do is to identify a sound pattern as being similar to one he heard before. As children develop their world model, the identities of objects and events become associated with impressions from all the available senses. To promote recognition via hearing, we need to ensure that sound plays its proper role in this process; that sound is associated with all other ways of knowing about the world.

Implications

One of the most effective ways to promote recognition via hearing is for the child to generate sound herself. Noise-making toys are a good start. But these should include toys in which the sound is directly related to the child's movement; things she can hit, bang, shake, and so forth. Pushing a button on an electronic device can entertain the child but it doesn't provide the same learning potential. And remember that any object is a toy for a child. Pan lids are good noise makers and spoons are good hammers. When the child is directly engaged in a noise-making activity, all senses are involved. The child sees and feels the action as well as hearing the results. She also receives proprioceptive feedback from muscles and joints (Figure 9–1). The movements and their sensory results

Figure 9–1. Tiffany is learning about hammering and she is associating it with sensations from hearing, vision, touch, movement, and proprioception. She is preparing the way for recognizing the event of hammering from sound alone.

become associated with the objects and events involved. In time, the child will be able recognize the events from sound alone when produced by another person—or by a sound recording device.

There are, of course, many sounds to be recognized that the child cannot make herself, such as the sound of a bird singing, a blender running, or thunder. Here, the important association is between sound and vision, sound and feeling, or sound and explanation. The child needs to see the objects involved and, if possible, the events they are engaged in. Fortunately, the consistent wearing of sensory assistance, and maintenance of the best possible hearing capacity, serve the child well. If he is also in an environment that is enriched in term of its potential to promote cognitive development, the necessary sound associations will follow. To the extent that help is needed, the adult can provide it by drawing the child's attention to the sound and its source, showing his or her own interest in it, and talking about it. Once the child has established a category for the event in his developing world model, he will begin to recognize it from hearing alone.

At this point, we must stress the importance of variety in the sound experiences. Part of the perceptual learning process requires that the child be exposed to the many ways in which a given event can produce sound patterns. Recorded examples in which each experience produces an identical sound can be entertaining but they deprive the child of the opportunity to learn the possible range of variation.

The Localization Principle

Rationale

Our ability to figure out precisely where a sound is coming from depends on input from two ears. The brain compares the two sensations and looks for discrepancies of amplitude, time, and spectrum. This information is used to determine direction and may also provide clues to distance. If we have to rely on only one ear, the brain can look for changes of amplitude or spectrum as we move or turn the head but the results are much poorer than those obtained with two ears. If the sound source is fixed and we already know where it is, then recognition automatically involves localization. Naturally, this only works for sources in fixed locations (e.g., a door knocker, or stove).

Implications

The obvious implication is that the child should be provided with sensory assistance in both ears. This can take the form of two hearing aids, two implants, or an aid in one ear and an implant in the other. There are times, of course, when this is impractical or undesirable and the child must rely on only one ear. And, even if the child has assisted hearing in both ears, there is no guarantee that the two sensations will provide the brain with the detailed information it needs to determine the direction of a sound source. Nevertheless, the child should be engaged in activities that help her realize that she can not only identify a sound but also figure out where it comes from. Her localization abilities will become apparent from her responses. At first, alerting may be accompanied by visual searching for the source of sound. When the child turns immediately to look in the direction of the sound this will be evidence of emerging localization skills. If she does so only because she already knows where the sound must be coming from, don't be concerned. The important thing is that she is using sound both for identifying events and for obtaining information about space.

Some Things to Remember

The goals of listening skills management are to ensure that the child:

1. Is **alerted** by sound,

2. Pays **attention** to sound and its details,

3. **Recognizes** sound,

4. And, if possible, uses sound for **space perception**.

Activities to promote attainment of these goals can include:

1. The child **making** the sound himself,

2. **Drawing** his attention to sound and **showing** him the source,

3. And ensuring that he hears **natural variations** in the sounds produced by a given event.

To Learn More

■ We have no specific suggestions for readings on promoting general listening skills. Because of the importance of spoken language acquisition, most texts that deal with listening skills do so in relation to the sounds of speech. We address that topic later.

■ In the meantime, we suggest that the more general use of hearing for learning about events in the environment and its incorporation into perceptual-cognitive development provide the underpinnings for the use of hearing to alert to, attend to, recognize, and interpret the events of spoken language.

CHAPTER 10

Spoken Language

We now focus on the aspects of intervention designed to promote spoken language development. For children with normal hearing, the process requires no special effort. They acquire spoken language skills spontaneously by listening to, and interacting with, fluent speakers of that language. Our concern, however, is children with hearing loss. In the previous two chapters, we outlined ways of bringing hearing capacity and hearing skill to their best possible level in spite of the loss. Unfortunately, the result falls short of normal by an amount that differs from child to child. The deficit is manifested in two ways. First, the child using a hearing aid or implant cannot hear the quietest sounds that are available to the child with normal hearing. As a result, he has reduced exposure to the speech going on in his environment. Second, even when sounds are loud enough to be heard, they lack clarity; the sound sensation is out of focus. One consequence of the loss of clarity is an increased susceptibility to the interfering effects of noise, which further restricts the child's access to the speech going on around him. These deficits may be further complicated by delays in acquiring hearing assistance, leading to further delays while the child learns to make sense of the new hearing. By themselves, the hearing deficits constitute a threat to the speed and quality of spoken language development.

But the child is not alone in this endeavor. Parents react both to the fact of the hearing loss and to any expected or observed effects on development. For some, the result is a reduction of verbal interaction with the child, adding to the negative effects of his hearing deficit when, in fact, the child needs more verbal interaction. These threats must be recognized and addressed if the child is to acquire age-appropriate spoken language skills.

153

It is, of course, the child who does the learning but the adults with whom he interacts can enrich his environment and experiences to promote that learning. Verbal interactions should account for the many nested levels of spoken language with constant attention to its communicative function. Maintaining hearing capacity at a consistent level enables hearing to play its natural, and critical, role. Cognitive development provides the foundation for language, and social cognition the foundation for communication. Play is the principal context for development in both areas and progress is best when the adults around the child are fluent users of the language to be learned.

Guiding Principles

The challenge is to take what is known about child development in general, and language development in particular, and to apply it in ways that will counteract the negative effects of the hearing loss. As in previous chapters, we suggest some basic principles and discuss their implications for intervention. In this case, we offer seven principles.

1. **The learner principle.** The task of learning falls to the child. The adults' responsibility is to create conditions and experiences that will speed and optimize learning.

2. **The nested principle.** Spoken language has many aspects that are nested within each other. It is counterproductive to focus on only one or two aspects and ignore others.

3. **The hearing principle.** Hearing is key to spoken language development. It is the sense that allows the child to control his own speech and to compare it with the speech produced by others. It is also the primary sense by which the spoken language of others is experienced.

4. **The cognition principle.** Language refers to what we know. Without cognition, there can be no language.

5. **The play principle**. Play is the primary context for cognitive and language learning in the young child. In a sense, play is the "work" of early childhood.

6. **The social-cognition principle.** Just as there can be no language without cognition, there can be no communication without social cognition.

7. **The fluency principle.** Language is best learned among people who are already fluent users of that language.

The Learner Principle

Rationale

Fortunately, children are born learners. The drive to learn and adapt is innate, as are the basic elements needed to satisfy this drive. These elements include sensory capacity, motor capacity, learning capacity, and an instinctive desire to interact with and understand the world of things, and the world of people (see Chapter 4). These drives, capacities, and desires provide the "nature" component of learning. But successful learning also requires a "nurture" component; that is, an environment with the necessary materials, objects, people, experiences, challenges, rewards, stimuli, and language. This environment must also provide opportunities for initiation, interaction, and exploration on the part of the child. The adults' role is to provide such an environment—to create the stage on which the child can best perform the act of learning.

Implications

There are many implications of this simple premise. First, one must trust the child's inherent desire and capacity for learning while taking account of his strengths, limitations, current attainments, readiness, and interest. The process must be child-centered; not curriculum-centered.

A second implication is the need to recognize that the child's primary learning environment is created by the parents. Therapy and preschool environments will become increasingly important as the child grows and matures. At that stage, the professional's intervention in the child's development is direct — he or she interacts with the child. At all stages, however, a key role of the professional is to help parents adapt the family environment to meet the child's learning needs. In this sense, the professional's intervention in the child's development is indirect; he or she interacts with the parents. But parents also have strengths and limitations and they are engaged in their own learning and development. These factors must be taken into account. The professional's words and actions in this context must be family-centered; not curriculum-centered.

A third implication is the need for observation. Professional intervention, whether direct or indirect, must be preceded by careful observation and assessment. Only when the professional has an understanding of the strengths and limitations of the child, the parents, their relationships and their interactions, will he or she be able to determine when intervention is needed, when it is not needed, what form it should take, and when it may be needed but is premature, inappropriate, or potentially counterproductive. In spite of commonalities, every child is unique and every family is unique. The professional needs to know them both before presuming to intervene. Even then, he or she should intervene cautiously, with empathy and respect.

The Nested Principle

Rationale

Spoken language development occurs at four main levels:

1. **Phonology**—the system of basic movement and sound patterns that are used to build words and sentences.

2. **Vocabulary**—the words that are used to refer to people, places, things, events, attributes, concepts, feelings, and relationships.

3. **Grammar**—rules by which words are selected, modified, and combined to create meaningful sentences.

4. **Pragmatics**—rules for the use of language to satisfy communicative intent and to meet social and cultural expectations.

Note that each level involves both perception (recognizing and understanding the speech of others) and production (generating speech that is recognizable and understandable by others).

These levels are nested like Russian nesting dolls. There are sounds within words, words within sentences, sentences within communication, and communication within a social context. In terms of development, the levels are somewhat sequential: Babbling with recognizable sounds comes before the first word; Single word utterances come before multiword sentences; and the ability to create multiword sentences provides a big boost to the development of pragmatic skills. But the levels also overlap. Even when babbling, the infant learns that his efforts influence others and he begins to use vocalization for purposeful communication, laying the foundation for conversation. Even at the single-word stage, the utterances communicate meaning and are, essentially, one-word sentences. And, when the child is combining words to make more complex sentences, he is still refining his phonology, expanding his vocabulary, learning new grammatical rules, and learning more effective ways to use language to satisfy communicative intent.

This nested structure provides a fine example of the developmental benefits of positive feedback in which effects reinforce their own cause. Increasing competence at any level not only creates readiness for higher levels but also reinforces the lower level skills on which it depends. For examples, new words provide the building blocks for more complex sentences while enhancing phonological development. Mastery of English plurals makes for more effective communication while refining the production of the "s" and "z" sounds.

Implications

Adults should recognize that language learning is taking place at many levels simultaneously and they should interact with the child accordingly. In particular, they should avoid focusing on one level to the exclusion or detriment of others. They should not, for example, insist on perfect articulation, the right word, correct grammar, or the polite form while ignoring a child's communicative efforts. It is important to repeat a child's message so that she hears it in a more complete, correct, or acceptable form, but it is equally important to respond to the meaning and intent, thereby reinforcing and encouraging learning at a communicative and pragmatic level.

Most parents instinctively respond to and interact with their children in ways that foster language development at many levels simultaneously. These instincts, however, can be undermined when the parents of a child with hearing loss are uncertain about the child's needs or their ability to meet them. Parents of children with hearing loss sometimes need encouragement, reassurance, support, demonstration, and/or coaching in this area. The message they need to hear is that they should talk to their child just as they would if she heard normally; only more so.

The Hearing Principle

Rationale

If a child is going to develop language in its spoken form, her brain needs sensory input from the speech of others and sensory feedback from her own speech efforts. Even though assisted hearing falls short of normal, it is usually good enough to meet this need. This is especially true now that the cochlear implant has become a viable option for children with profound or total hearing loss. Note, also, that hearing is the *only* sense that gives the child access to her own speech and the speech of others in the same modality.

At this point, we need to say something about lipreading. In face-to-face communication, vision provides sensory access to

Nested Language Levels

Child: (touches mother's nose) No.

Mother: Yes, that's my nose. And that's your nose. Where's my mouth?

Child: (Touching) Maow.

Mother: Yes that's my mouth. Where is your mouth?

Child: (Touching self). Maow.

Mother: Yes that's your mouth.

Child: (Tiring of game and wriggling) Dau.

Mother: You want to get down. OK. Down you go. (Puts child down).

■ This simple exchange exposes the child to sounds he has not yet mastered (phonology).

■ However imperfect his production, he is learning to use words conceptually for classes of objects (vocabulary).

■ Although he is at the one-word stage, he is being exposed to simple sentences that include words such as "where," "my," and "your" that he has yet to master (vocabulary and grammar).

■ The exchange has all the hallmarks of conversation including turn-taking, several turns on the same topic, and a change of topic (pragmatics).

■ In this case the child initiated the change of topic (pragmatics).

■ Mother responded to his intent, providing reinforcement. The learning potential of this exchange would have been severely reduced if the mother had interrupted it at any point to insist on better articulation, or if she had ignored the child's wishes to change topic.

some of the movement patterns of speech. These include movements of the lips, the jaw, and, to a limited extent, the front of the
tongue. In many situations, lipreading can serve as a valuable supplement by providing clues to details that are not heard. Lipreading
cannot, however, be a complete substitute for hearing in the developing child for one simple reason: most of the key movements of
speech are invisible. This limitation includes all of the movements
that actually generate sound and most of the movements that shape
the spectrum of sound on its way out of the mouth (see Chapter 2).
Note also that, unless the child is watching herself in a mirror, she
does not see her own speech movements and, therefore, has no way
to compare her own speech with that of others. These statements
may seem at odds with the fact that there are some individuals who
can lipread with great ease and with no help from hearing. But
these are not developing children. They are older children or adults
who have already developed considerable world, social, and language knowledge and are unusually adept at using this knowledge
to compensate for the information that cannot be seen or heard.

Implications

One obvious implication of the hearing principle is the need for
early, optimal, and consistent provision of hearing assistance followed by the development of basic hearing skills, as discussed in
Chapters 8 and 9.

A second implication, especially for the infant, is the need to
hear as much speech as possible. Parents can keep up a running
commentary during play and the activities of everyday living. It is
not important that the child understand what is being said. He just
needs to hear lots of spoken language, preferably related to what he
is experiencing. For the toddler, bedtime stories and other rituals
provide excellent contexts for speech input and they do so at close
distance where the negative effects of noise and reverberation are
minimal (see Chapters 1 and 8).

A third implication is that the child needs to hear herself in
order to establish the connections between speech movement and
speech sound. Anything that involves and promotes babbling and

vocal interaction will help. Conversations, however rudimentary, provide equal opportunities for the child to hear her own speech and that of the communication partner.

Hearing Speech

■ Daddy is bouncing baby Karen on his knee. As the two gaze at each other in mutual adoration, daddy talks and sings songs indigenous to the family culture (Figure 10–1). "Pop goes the weasel" is a great hit as he gives her a big bounce on the last line. At the end of the song, the child wriggles and vocalizes, indicating she wants a repetition. She is not only using voice for communication but also engaging in the rudiments of conversation. At some point, she imitates the word "pop" as well as she can. Daddy responds with evident surprise and pleasure and repeats, "Yes, POP goes the weasel."

■ James is sitting in his high chair, waiting for lunch. Big brother Tommy is teaching James finger games that he learned at school: Eentsy Weenstsy spider and Pat-a-Cake. They take turns singing and Tommy tries to correct James's mistakes.

■ Mommy is changing William's diaper. "OK. Here we go. What do we have in here? Yuk! So much poop. Let's get rid of that. Now we can clean you up. Doesn't that feel better? And here's a nice clean diaper. One. Two. All done. OK! Let's see what's for lunch."

The nature of the activity is not important. What is important is that it engages the child and provides an opportunity for hearing speech, both self-generated and generated by others. Moreover, the speech is generated at close quarters where the effects of distance, noise, and reverberation are minimal. Had Daddy just bounced Karen, or Mommy changed William, in silence, or if his brother had been off doing his own thing while James waited patiently for lunch, opportunities to hear speech would have been lost. (The same would be true if the children were not wearing their hearing aids or implants, or if the batteries were dead).

Figure 10–1. "Pop" goes the weasel.

Although our concern is with hearing, there is no good reason to deprive the child of the opportunity to see the talker's face. Lip-reading and hearing do not compete, but are different sources of information about the same speech events. Moreover, it is important for the child to see and interpret the emotional expressions that accompany speech (see Figure 10–1). Once the child is developing vocabulary, there may be occasions when it is appropriate to focus the child's attention on the sounds of speech without supplementing them with vision. This can be done in a natural way by speaking when the child is looking elsewhere or by speaking from the side rather than the front, as shown in Figure 10–2.

The Cognition Principle

Rationale

The words of language are symbols. They stand for something else. Their value is that they stand for something that is known to

Figure 10–2. Talking from the side gives June a chance to process speech by hearing only. If she needs lipreading assistance she can easily turn to look at the face of the talker.

the listener. Some words refer to specific objects or events such as "Mummy," "Daddy," "Mary," "me," "up," and "Bye bye." Between 2 and 4 years of age, however, a great transformation takes place. Words become symbols for concepts. They are general purpose symbols that can be used for anything that falls within the child's understanding of the concept. For example, the word "mummy" in "Is that Sally's mummy?" conveys the child's knowledge about family relationships as they apply to someone outside the immediate family.

As pointed out in Chapter 4, we tend to classify words according to the type of category to which they refer. Nouns refer to categories of objects (cat, person, tree, etc.). Adjectives refer to categories of object-properties (blue, big, hot, etc.). Verbs refer to categories of events (walk, hit, fall, etc.). Adverbs refer to categories of event-properties (slow, quick, sudden, etc.). And prepositions refer to categories of space- and time-properties (near, far, on, under, inside, before, after, etc.). In other words, the symbols of language stand for things the child "knows" about space, time, things, events, their properties, and their relationships; that is, cognition. When words are selected, modified, and combined to create a sentence, the meaning of that sentence is also drawn from the child's evolving world model.

Cognition provides the basis for language but, once established, language becomes a powerful tool for further cognitive development. The child learns from verbal interactions with other people. At this point, cognitive development is no longer tied to the here and now. There can be conversations about distant, past, future, abstract, and hypothetical things and events. This is another example of the power of positive feedback in which an outcome enhances its own cause. Cognition leads to language, which promotes cognition, which leads to more language, which enhances cognition, and so on. The intimate and interdependent relationship between thinking and language has challenged philosophers for many years. Is language just thinking out loud, or do we actually need language to think? In terms of the relationship between cognition and language in early development, however, there can be no doubt that cognition comes first. Without cognition, there can be no language—there is nothing to which language can refer. Parrots can talk but they do not have language.

Implications

We suggest three implications of the cognition principle. First, by enriching the child's early environment and experiences in ways that promote, speed, and enhance cognitive development, we lay the foundation for language. To put it simply, the more the child knows, the more he will have to talk about when he is ready to speak. For the infant, this means providing lots of materials and toys with which to interact and lots of problems to solve. Interaction with things having different shapes, colors, textures, and noise-making properties allows the evolving concepts to become associated with sight, sound, touch, movement, and proprioception.

More About Words

As indicated in Chapter 4, early words in a child's vocabulary refer to specific objects, events, or persons in his immediate environment. As he acquires concepts, he will often use these words in a more general sense. One sees this happening when the new language learner first refers to an adult male stranger as "Dada." He is taking an old label, which served him well as a referent for one person. and applying it to the general category of adult male. He has yet to learn the label "man." To take another example, "chair" no longer refers only to the infant's own high chair but to all objects that fulfill the function of a chair. In this case, however, he doesn't need a new word.

At around 18 months, Peter was taken on a trip to the zoo. On seeing the ears, eyes, and nostrils of a submerged hippopotamus he pointed and said "frog!" He already had a concept of a class of creatures that deserved the label "frog" and this creature seemed to meet some of their characteristics. This was an opportunity to expand both his world model and his vocabulary.

Even when the child has reached the stage of using words as labels for conceptual categories, he is still faced with the challenge of communicating about specifics. This is when he discovers the power of the sentence as in, "Where my blue ball?" The general purpose "ball" has been given the power to apply to a specific instance by virtue of its relationship to other words in the sentence.

The second implication is that the language used with the child should relate to what she is doing, what she is attending to, or what she is thinking about. Even for the infant who can understand nothing of what is being said, there are potential benefits to making connections between the language and whatever is occupying the child's attention (Figure 10–3).

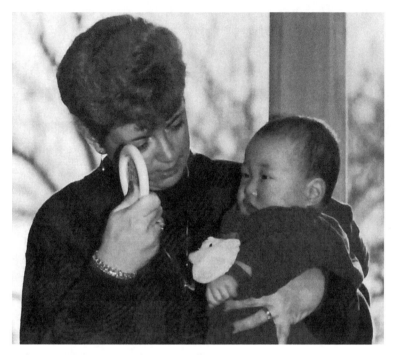

Figure 10–3. Jean is talking to Karen about the object that is holding her attention. The fact that she does not understand is irrelevant at this stage.

The third implication is that, when evaluating the child's progress, one should pay less attention to the number of sounds and words she can produce or the length and grammatical accuracy of her sentences but be more concerned about her understanding of what the words refer to and what the sentences mean.

The Play Principle

Rationale

There are two main contexts for cognitive and language learning in young children. First, there are the activities of everyday living.

These are usually parent-directed and have an obvious goal such as dressing, bathing, toileting, and feeding. Second, there is play, which is usually more child-directed. The boundary between the activities of everyday living and play are often blurred, as when the child plays with toys in the bathtub or food at the table. In a sense, everything is play to the young child; play is the work of childhood. Parents can take advantage of the child's instincts for play by introducing playlike elements into the activities of everyday living. Play increases the opportunities for the child to experience, experiment with, and explore the world, while building an internal model of it.

When child-directed, play can be solitary or shared. Solitary play may not advance language but it can certainly advance cognition, providing a richer world model to which language can later refer. Play shared with an adult has the potential to advance both cognition and language. At the same time, it can promote learning in the areas of social cognition and the pragmatic aspects of communication. From the child's point of view, interaction with adults is sometimes a primary motivation for play. The child may well be interested in the content of a book, for example, but the opportunity to interact with an adult can be a major motivating factor (Figure 10–4). The same can be said about puzzles and board games.

The form taken by play depends on the developmental level of the child. During the first few months his focus is on control of his own body. He turns his head, moves his limbs, focuses, gazes, rolls over, and eventually sits up. Around 6 months of age, he sits unsupported and can now focus on control of objects by manipulation. At the same time, he becomes increasingly aware of the properties of objects and their similarities and differences (Figure 10–5). His vocalizations also mature into babbling, in which he assimilates and explores the sounds of the language he has been hearing. Pretty soon, he learns to control his position in space by crawling and, at around 1 year of age by walking. This is also the time when he begins to produce one-word sentences and he discovers the power of language as a means of controlling adults; he progresses from the Spoon game to the "Why?" game (see "Games for Control of Adults" below).

Figure 10–4. Reading together can promote auditory, cognitive, and language learning while meeting the child's desire for interaction with adults.

Figure 10–5. Colin considers similarities and differences.

Games for Control of Adults

The Spoon game

The child is holding his spoon but, at this stage of development, he is not an effective user. However, the spoon is good for banging on the tray of his high chair and it makes a great sound. At some point he loses control of the spoon and it falls on the floor. The adult then picks it up and replaces it on the tray. From the child's point of view, the spoon is no longer just a tool for making noise but also seems to have great potential for controlling adults. To test this hypothesis, he throws it on the floor again, and again, and again. This is a wonderful example of the child's emerging cognitive and social development. It is also a great opportunity for appropriate language input.

The "Why?" game

Once children acquire a concept of cause and effect, and the language to go with it, they usually discover the power of "Why?" For one thing, it prompts the adult to provide information and promotes verbally mediated cognitive development. But the child soon finds that it is a powerful tool for maintaining interaction. It is the verbal equivalent of the spoon game. Although it can sometimes be exasperating, indulge the child—at least for a while.

By around 2 years of age, children have organized their world model conceptually, and language development accelerates. Further evidence for this change comes in the form of increased involvement in symbolic play. The playthings are no longer just objects in their own right but become symbols for something else. As such, they provide a parallel to language. A toy car can represent a real car just as the word "car" can refer to an actual car. The symbolic aspect becomes more pronounced when the play object doesn't look like the real object. A building block, for example, can represent a horse, a car, an airplane, or any other class of object in the child's world model. Solitary symbolic play gives the child an opportunity to explore this inner world of concepts. Shared symbolic play has the additional benefit of allowing an adult partner to introduce appropriate language. If, for example, the child is obviously playing with a block as if it were an airplane, words such as "airplane," "fly," and "sky" become appropriate, even though the objects and actions to which they would normally refer are not present. Symbolic play becomes a bridge to the use of language in that it, too, escapes the limits of the here and now.

Implications

The first implication is that the playthings available to the child should support cognitive growth. Many toy distributors provide ratings for the learning potential of their products, categorized according to age. A good measure of learning potential is the extent to which the toy requires the child to solve problems. The postal shape box is a good example. Objects with various three-dimensional shapes can only be put in the box through an aperture with the corresponding two-dimensional cross-section.

The second implication is that parents should play with their child as much as possible. The nature of the play, and the objects involved, should again support cognitive growth but should be accompanied by appropriate language. As the child develops, the language can become part of the cognitive process via instructions and questions (e.g., "Find me a wheel" or "What do we need here?"). Jigsaw puzzles are an excellent medium for promoting fine-motor control, perceptual awareness of similarities and differences, and problem-solving. The adult's language can relate both to the content of the picture being assembled and the process of assembling it (e.g., "The horse still needs legs," "We want a piece with red on it," or "I think that piece is too big").

During the activities of everyday living there are many opportunities for play and problem-solving. We can play "hide the soap" or "sink the boats," for example, or "find all the yellow M&Ms."

Buttons, zippers, snaps, and Velcro fasteners also offer problems to be solved while promoting fine motor development.

The general message for parents is to play with the child and to do so in ways that promote cognitive development and enhance problem-solving skills. At the same time, they should provide the language that goes with the activities and, when the child is ready, use language as a component of play.

These implications, of course, can be applied to children with normal hearing. What is different for children with hearing loss is an increased need for interactive play that serves to promote both cognitive and language development.

The Social-Cognition Principle

Rationale

Just as general cognition underlies language, so social cognition underlies communication. Social cognition refers to what the child "knows" about the world of people; how people look, behave, feel, think, and react; and how they convey their intentions. As with general cognition, much of this knowledge is implicit rather than explicit. In the first few months of life, babies become aware of the world as something separate from themselves, and they become aware of people as a special class of objects. Between 6 and 12 months, they learn that there are differences between the properties of people and the properties of things. In particular they learn that the control of people is different from the manipulation of things. They also begin to show preference for familiar people and wariness, or even fear, of strangers. Once they master locomotion, they continue to use familiar people as a secure base from which to explore. Between 2 and 4 years, children begin to acquire concepts for internal events such as remembering, knowing, thinking, wanting, feeling, hurting, liking, disliking, and owning. At this stage, they are acquiring a Theory of Mind, as outlined in Chapter 4. They begin to appreciate that other people share a model of the physical and social world but that there can also be differences. Advances in social cognition are accompanied by the use of more complicated language structures related to cause/effect relationships.

Implications

The primary implication is that the child should be provided with ample opportunity to observe, interact, and play with adults and other children. Unless the child has an additional impairment related to social function, there is no need to structure these inter-actions any differently from those experienced by the child with normal hearing.

A second implication is that, once the child is using language as a medium for learning, parents should include vocabulary related to social cognition and internal "events" such as feelings, perceptions, motivation, and reasoning.

Language and Social Cognition

Joan sees Mary crying and looks at her mother with a puzzled expression.

Mother responds with, "Mary is crying *because* she is *unhappy*. She really *wanted* an ice cream and her mommy said No. I think her mommy said No *because* she *thinks if* Mary eats the ice cream, *then* she won't eat her dinner."

Note use of the words "unhappy," "want," and "think" that are related to internal processes in another person and the words "because" and "if-then" that are related, here, to cause and effect relationships in another person.

A third implication is that adult interactions should take account of the social-cognitive developmental level of the child. When a baby is observed to show fear or wariness of strangers, for exam-ple, a professional attempting interaction should maintain physical distance until the child makes a social overture. This may come in the form of relaxing, smiling, establishing eye contact, reaching, moving closer, or offering or accepting a toy or other object.

Toddlers are able to move away from familiar caregivers to explore the world beyond them, but the caregivers should be aware of their role as a secure base from which the child can explore. Social referencing, joint eye contact, and response to voice all serve to establish psychological and emotional contact in lieu of physical contact. At the toddler stage, a lot of time is spent in restricting exploration in the interests of safety. It is good to child-proof the house but it is also a time to promote social cognition as the child learns that restriction and protection can go hand in hand. Just saying, "No! Stop! Don't!" may serve the purpose of protection but it misses a good opportunity to associate restriction with parental concern as the dominating principle.

Another major social-cognitive concept at this age is that of ownership. Children often take a toy or book from another child with tearful consequences. This is the time to learn that other children also have a sense of ownership. As with other aspects of development, the parents of a child with hearing loss do not need to act differently from the way they would if their child had normal hearing. They just need to acknowledge the wishes, rights, feelings, and beliefs of each participant in the tussle and provide the appropriate language.

By preschool age, children have established both autonomy and mobility. They are developing a sense of self and sorting out what, about them, is the same as, or different from, others. Much of their social cognition is now acquired through cooperative play. The expanded social context includes individuals with a variety of roles: teachers, therapists, teaching assistants, bus drivers, secretaries, and so forth. It is important that the child be exposed to the language associated with this expanded social context. Parents can play a role here but only if they are familiar with school routines, classmates, and the various adults with whom the child is now interacting. This requires classroom observation and establishing a close parent-teacher relationship. Teacher-made books about classroom routines that are illustrated with pictures and new vocabulary can be helpful to parents. Similarly, pictures from home can be shared with teachers and classmates (Figure 10–6). Children can be encouraged to convey their social understanding of the world of school by drawing pictures, telling stories about their day, or answering direct questions. The child's report helps convey his understanding of the social reality of his expanding world. Any incongruity between the adult's and the child's understanding is a glorious opportunity for exploration through the language of social cognition.

Earlier, we pointed out that, although language emerges from cognition, once developed, it becomes a powerful tool for enhancing cognition. This is particularly true with social cognition. The language related to personal characteristics, roles, feelings, motivation, and so on becomes key to the child's establishment of an understanding of the world of people and her ability to communicate with others.

Figure 10–6. "Who's that?" "It's my Mommy." (Photograph courtesy of Clarke Schools for Hearing and Speech.)

A Question of Roles

A preschool class was run by a teaching team made up of a deaf educator, an early childhood educator, a teaching assistant, and a speech pathologist. The teacher of the deaf and early childhood teacher were in the classroom all the time and shared authority. One of the teachers was a first-year teacher and new to the classroom. The other had been at the school for a long time and assumed more of a leadership role during the first few weeks. William, a 4-year-old, with hearing loss said to the first-year teacher, "Who's the boss in here?" The teacher answered, "We're a team; there are two leaders." The boy said, "Yeah, but who's the one in charge?" He may have been reporting a notion of how classrooms work from earlier experience. Or, he may have observed the way the teacher roles were actually being carried out. Whatever, the reason, it was an opportunity to recognize and verbalize the child's understanding of his observation and to talk about why the teachers were doing the job the way he observed. The response was, "We're both here to help you learn. We take turns helping you to learn in the classroom."

Note:

- William's drive to acquire social cognition is what prompts this exchange.

- The thoughtful response reinforces that drive.

- William has an opportunity to modify his concept of "One class, one boss."

- Language is being used to reinforce a drive that contributed to communicative development in the first place—yet another example of positive feedback.

The Fluency Principle

Rationale

The goal of providing an enriched environment in which the child can acquire spoken language skills is undermined if the language used among family members is different from that used with him. It is further undermined if the language used with him has a restricted vocabulary, and limited grammar. This issue becomes a problem when the parents are not fluent in the dominant language of the culture, especially if that is the language that will be used in school.

Implications

There are no simple solutions to the problems caused by differences among the language of home, the language of school, and the language of society at large. In the early stages of development, the interests of cognitive, linguistic, and social-emotional development are best met when parents and other family members interact with the child in the same language they use with each other. Once the child has reached a certain level of competence, it may be appropriate to add exposure to the dominant language of the culture. But decisions about mechanisms and timing must be based on the child's hearing and language skills, the fluency and competence of family members in both languages, and the availability of other adults who are fluent in the language of the dominant culture.

The relationship between signed and spoken languages comes up in this context. Signed languages have the virtue of being fully accessible by vision. Deaf children born to signing deaf parents acquire signed language skills naturally and spontaneously. Because of the importance of language and the intimate relationship between cognition and language, it is sometimes suggested that

A Story of Limited Fluency

Juliana was born with a profound hearing loss. Her hearing parents decided to learn sign language to use with her until she was old enough to receive a cochlear implant. This decision was based on recognition of Juliana's need to be exposed to a rich language system during the waiting period. Although Juliana was fit with appropriate binaural hearing aids at 6 weeks of age, her auditory access to speech was limited. A deaf American Sign Language (ASL) instructor came to the house weekly to teach the family to sign. Their emerging sign language was used when interacting with and caring for their daughter. A hearing teacher of the deaf also made weekly visits to the home to help Juliana use her hearing aids, develop listening skills, however limited, and prepare for adaptation to improved hearing once implanted. This second teacher was not fluent in ASL but was supportive of the parents' use of sign language. Arriving at the house for her weekly visit, the teacher of the deaf found the mother feeding her baby.

Mother: "You know it's hard to figure out how to sign meaningfully while feeding. I mean, I hold her with one arm and use the other hand to hold the bottle. It doesn't leave an extra hand for communication."

Teacher: "That's because you are not deaf. If signing was your native language, you would sign into your baby's bottom with the hand that is supporting her. She would be bathed in language the way parents shower their hearing babies with spoken language long before they understand it."

Eventually, Juliana received binaural implants and developed age-appropriate spoken language skills. It is difficult to know how much the early exposure to imperfect ASL contributed to her later progress but it certainly did not hurt.

the hearing parents of deaf children should learn sign language and use it to interact with the child. This recommendation carries considerable weight when the child is profoundly or totally deaf and must wait until he is 12 months of age before acquiring implanted hearing. The obvious problem, however, is that the parents, even when highly motivated, are unlikely to acquire fluency in sign or to use it for communication with each other and other family members. The imaginative and appropriate use of gestures and signs can supplement the limited information available via hearing aids and help build some of the foundations of communication when auditory access to spoken language is poor. They will not, however, contribute to phonological development. Fortunately, there are numerous examples of profoundly deaf children who have developed excellent spoken language skills, including phonology, in spite of delays of 1, 2, or 3 years before receiving cochlear implants.

Some Additional Thoughts

1. Everything said so far has been based on the assumption that hearing loss is the child's only impairment. Unfortunately, some 30 to 40% of children with hearing loss must develop and learn with one or more additional impairments. When these impairments are of perceptual or motor function, they will interfere with establishment of the hearing and speech skills needed for the development of phonology. Impairments of cognitive function undermine the very foundation of language. And deficits of social cognition, as in autistic spectrum disorders, undermine the drive for communication and, therefore, reduce the child's need for language. The presence of additional disorders does not change the basic principles outlined here, or their implications, but it does increase the challenges of management. It also calls for exceptional observational, diagnostic, and intervention skill on the part of clinicians and

teachers and it increases the need for effective collaboration among professionals from a variety of disciplines. Because of newborn screening, however, it is often the professional specializing in deafness who first observes developmental patterns suggesting the presence of a secondary impairment.

2. Much of what we have said in this chapter comes from a body of knowledge in child development and, therefore, can be applied to children in general. In fact, we are proposing that the ideal learning environment for the child with hearing loss is also an ideal learning environment for a normally hearing, typically developing child. It was just such a realization on the part of Maria Montessori that led to the development of educational programs for normally developing children that were based on techniques found to be effective with developmentally delayed children. It is important to realize, however, that the normally hearing, typically developing child can learn well in a less than ideal learning environment whereas the child with hearing loss cannot. Speaking metaphorically, the normally hearing, typically developing child can, if he must, learn from the crumbs that fall from the table. But the child with hearing loss, or any other impairment that threatens development, needs to be seated at the table.

3. We have already stressed the importance of social cognition. We have spoken of it, however, only as that part of the child's world model relating to people, their special properties, and their special cause-effect relationships. Social-emotional function, however, is not limited to what the child knows about the world of people but also how he feels about it and how he relates to it. It also includes how he feels about himself and how he perceives and responds to his own feelings. As indicated in Chapter 4, social-emotional function is one of the three principal supports of language development, the other two being cognitive and sensorimotor function. We deal with the enhancement of the child's environment and experiences to promote social-emotional development in the next chapter.

Some Things to Remember

This chapter has been about promoting the development of age-appropriate spoken language in the child with hearing loss. Based on observations of normal child development, we have made the following suggestions:

1. The goal is to **enhance** the child's environment, experiences, and language exposure in ways that will support her natural ability and desire for **learning**.

2. Professional Interaction with the child and the family should be based on knowledge gained through careful **observation**.

3. Language has many **nested** levels. Focusing on one to the exclusion of others is counterproductive.

4. Development will be better and faster to the extent that **hearing** can play its natural role.

5. **Cognitive development** provides the basis for language.

6. **Play** is the work of childhood. It is the primary context for cognitive, social cognitive, and language learning.

7. **Social cognition** provides the basis for communication.

8. In the early stages of development, it is important that parents interact with the child using a language in which they are comfortable and **fluent**.

9. These principles remain valid when there are **additional impairments**.

To Learn More

■ An excellent and accessible text on early cognitive and language development is *The Scientist in the Crib* (Gopnik, Meltzoff, & Kuhl, 1999). As pointed out in Chapter 4, the title refers both to the professionals who learn about child development by making, testing, and revising hypotheses to explain their observations, and to the child, who learns about her physical and social worlds in the same way.

- The same topic is covered, but with special emphasis on the role of play, in *Einstein Never Used Flash Cards* (Hirsh-Pasek & Golinkoff, 2003).

- For more reading in the area of language and language acquisition we recommend Language Acquisition (de Villiers & de Villiers, 1978).

- The process has not changed in the past 35 years but theories and descriptions have. For a more recent text on the same topic we suggest *Born to Talk: An Introduction to Speech and Language Development*, 5th Edition (Hulit & Fahey, 2010).

- More specifics on techniques and materials for speeding and optimizing language acquisition in children with special needs are provided in *The New Language of Toys: A Guide for Parents and Teachers* (Schwartz, 2003).

- A recent text dealing with intervention and hearing impairment is *Children with Hearing Loss: Developing Listening and Talking, Birth to Six* (Cole & Flexer, 2010). In addition to its own valuable content, this is an excellent source of references to the work of other teachers and researchers.

- For professionals who are looking for guidance in adapting early childhood programs to meet the needs of children with hearing loss, we recommend nine booklets published by the National Association of the Education of Young Children (NAEYC). These booklets address Standards and Criteria specific to NAEYC and describe a process of accreditation that involves self-study. http://www.naeyc.org/academy .

- Mention was made earlier of the work of Maria Montessori in Italy. Early in the 20th century, she developed an educational program complete with philosophy, curriculum, materials, teaching methods, laboratory schools, and teacher-training institutes. This was originally developed for children who were not learning in traditional schools. The philosophy was based on observations of the growth and development of young children and a belief that learning should be self-directed (the Learner principle). Her programs produced children who were competent learners but a rigid and doctrinaire application of her philosophy and methods came under criticism in the 1930s and 1940s. Since that time, Montessori programs have been successfully adapted for use in the United States and are currently found in private and public educational settings. For an introduction to Montessori, her philosophy and methods, we suggest the abridged and annotated edition of her own text *The Montessori Method* edited by Gutek (2004). Insights into Montessori's philosophy in someone else's words will be found in *Montessori in the Classroom: A Teacher's Account of How Children Really Learn* (Lillard, 1997).

▪ Another interesting approach to early education also comes from Italy. Loris Malaguzzi and parents from villages in the region of Reggio Emilia developed community-based early childhood programs after World War II. The programs were designed to provide children with a sound intellectual background in thinking, creative expression, communication, and community. The concept was of an enriched environment based on the interests of the children so that they could take full advantage of public school in their later years. The philosophy became known as the Reggio Emilia Approach and has been adopted by preschool programs around the world. As with Montessori, much has been written on this topic. We suggest starting with *The Reggio Approach: Bringing Learning to Life* (Caldwell, 2003).

▪ For readers who want to learn more about an approach to learning that uses scaffolding, mental tools, self-regulation activities, and reflective thinking, we suggest: *Tools of the Mind: The Vygotskian Approach to Early Childhood Education* (Bodrova & Leong, 2006).

CHAPTER 11

Social-Emotional Function

All children have the same social and emotional needs: to develop attachment relationships with parents, other family members, and caregivers; to develop a healthy self-image; to build friendships; and to learn to use adults as a resource. For children with hearing loss, born into a hearing family, emotional well-being is at risk. The parents' inexperience with deafness, their feelings of inadequacy when facing the task of raising a child with hearing loss, and their initial emotional and intellectual reactions to the diagnosis can undermine their ability to meet the child's emotional needs. As the child grows, imperfect hearing and reduced language competence can limit the development of social competence. This problem is made worse in noisy classrooms where the poor acoustics add to the difficulty of gaining access to social situations and forming friendships. A primary goal of intervention is the development of age-appropriate spoken language. But pursuit of this goal without also attending to social-emotional needs is counterproductive. As we discussed in Chapters 4 and 10, social-emotional function provides the foundation for communication, which is the context in which spoken language is acquired and applied.

In this chapter, we identify some of the ways in which this aspect of development can be nurtured. In the infant, effective use of sound and hearing reduces surprise and anxiety by maintaining connection to people and events in the environment. If necessary, parents can learn to understand the benefits of clearly and consistently enforcing behavioral limits, and of acknowledging feelings, efforts, and accomplishments. As in Chapter 10, we emphasize that attempts to offer guidance to parents should be preceded by careful observation of child and family, preferably in the home. Once again, the most effective context for social-emotional development of the young child is play: solitary, parallel, shared with peers, shared with parents, or shared with professionals. In addition, children learn by example. Prosocial behavior in the adults with whom the child interacts can serve as a valuable model.

Definitions

The words used to talk about social-emotional development are often loosely defined. The following explains our use of key terms in this text.

1. **Emotion.** For present purposes, we define emotion as a sensation or feeling resulting from internal processes. Words used to refer to these feelings include confidence/fear, happiness/sadness, comfort/discomfort, pride/shame, love/hate, and anger. As you will see, many of these words suggest an emotional continuum ranging from the positive to the negative. Emotional reactions are often triggered by an obvious external event. Sometimes, however, internal factors such as history or neurological make up can contribute to an emotional response when a causal factor is not immediately obvious.

2. **Emotional function and development.** We define healthy emotional function as appropriate perception of, and interaction with, one's self. Emotional development involves learning to recognize, label, and express feelings; to make appropriate connections between these feelings and external causes; and to respond to negative emotions and their causes in ways that will move toward a more positive or balanced state. In this context, a positive emotional state is one that allows the individual to explore, take risks, and solve problems—behaviors that contribute to the development of the cognitive and social skills needed for interaction and communication.

3. **Social function and development.** We define healthy social function as appropriate perception of, and interaction with, others. This process requires social cognition, or an understanding of the social world, including a Theory of Mind, as discussed in Chapter 4. Social development also involves the acquisition of empathy, which we define as the ability to share the emotional reactions of others. It also involves learning the social rules of the culture and responding to social situations in ways that are culturally acceptable.

4. **Bonding.** Bonding refers to an initial primal emotional tie between a caregiver and a newborn.

5. **Attachment.** Whereas bonding is largely instinctive and immediate, attachment is an enduring emotional connection that develops over time.

More About Attachment and Bonding

As the terms are used here, attachment and bonding carry different implications. *Bonding* is fed largely by hormones and heightened sensory awareness. In adult relationships, bonding might be considered analogous to "falling in love." It is a relationship in which the participants still have limited knowledge and experience with each other. It is helpful, though not essential, in initiating the attachment involved in a long-term relationship. In contrast, *attachment* develops over time and is based on shared knowledge and experience. One characteristic of attachment is reciprocity which includes the ability to adjust to the actions and wishes of another while retaining one's own identity. It suggests a mutuality of control and influence in which neither party dominates. The locus of control shifts back and forth between the two. Reciprocity between a caregiver and child is demonstrated by matching and synchronous behaviors and by mutual delight and regulation of responses. Reciprocity is also a characteristic of friendships. Attachment, bonding, and reciprocity are all evidence of healthy social-emotional development.

Social and emotional development can be discussed independently but they are interdependent. Both begin with the relationship between child and primary caregiver. The importance of this interdependence was concisely expressed by Lee Travis, one of the founders of the profession of Speech/Language Pathology in the United States, when he said, of the developing child, "I am what I think you think I am."[1]

Guiding Principles

We suggest that positive social-emotional development of the child will be promoted when interactions follow these principles:

1. **The hearing principle.** Hearing can play a valuable role in the young child's understanding of himself and his physical and social world.

2. **The observation principle.** We already stressed the importance of observation as a precursor to intervention related to language. Careful observation is even more critical in relation to social-emotional development.

3. **The novelty principle.** Healthy social-emotional development requires a balance between the security and predictability of the familiar and the challenge of the novel.

4. **The limit principle.** Children need clear and consistent limits beyond which certain behaviors are not acceptable.

5. **The acknowledgment principle.** Children need acknowledgment and validation of feelings, intentions, wishes, efforts, and accomplishments.

6. **The play principle.** Interactive play provides a fruitful context for social-emotional development.

---

[1]A line used by Travis during a 1969 meeting in Minneapolis.

7. **The modeling principle.** Social-emotional development is nurtured when adults provide positive examples.

The Hearing Principle

Rationale

In primates, early attachments are formed, at first, through the senses of touch and vision. This is good news for hearing parents of children with hearing loss. Deaf children have full access to facial expressions, gestures, and tactile sensations. Their parents can be reassured that they are perfectly capable of interpreting and meeting the emotional needs of their new baby, even if he can't hear them. Once the child is provided with hearing assistance, however, sound can play a role in furthering attachment and reciprocity. Sound provides information about what adults are doing in the environment. Sounds of caregiving (food preparation, putting away baby clothes) let the baby know that the caregiver is present even when not in sight. Transitions in the environment always involve movement and are accompanied by sound. The sounds of a mother collecting keys, bottles, and toys in preparation for a trip, serve to prepare the baby for the upcoming change. Without them, transitions may be experienced as unexpected or capricious. The melody and cadence of a mother's voice convey her emotional state and help to regulate the emotional state of the child. Similarly, the child's responses to sound contribute to the development of trust on the part of parents as they learn they can provide comfort by talking or singing. The infant's differentiated utterances in the first few months of life contribute to reciprocity and turn-taking and interactions between child and adult that are enjoyable to both. These are the beginning stages of conversation. A parent's ability to interact with, monitor, and control her baby through the sense of hearing allows for connection to be maintained when the two cannot see each other.

Finally, the parent's knowledge that they share the child's sensory status allows for greater confidence that they will be able to anticipate and meet her needs. In summary, optimization of assisted hearing capacity and emergence of hearing skills engender positive reactions in both child and parents and serve to enhance their relationship. In this way, hearing contributes to the child's social-emotional development.

Implications

Healthy social-emotional development provides one more reason for optimizing hearing capacity and skill as early in the developmental process as possible. With the introduction of universal newborn hearing screening and developments in pediatric audiology, it has become possible to fit children with hearing aids by 3 months of age.

On the negative side, it has been suggested that attachment can be at risk if parents learn about the hearing loss before they have had a chance to form a bond with their new baby. Most professionals, however, believe that the developmental benefits of early diagnosis and intervention outweigh any negative effects. Many parents would agree with this conclusion, but perhaps not until they come to know their child and witness developmental progress.

A second implication returns us to the issue of consistency in the maintenance of best hearing capacity. If the child is to hear and learn to recognize the activities of other people in the environment, especially those that signal an approaching adult or an imminent change, she must be wearing her hearing aids or cochlear implant processors and they must be maintained in full working order.

Parents can also help by making noises that will provide the child with sensory evidence about what is going on around him. The simple act of talking to the child while approaching the nursery door can keep the child in touch with the social environment.

The Way It Was

Before newborn hearing screening became standard, the first cue to hearing loss often came when parents became suspicious because of absent or inconsistent responses to sound. There was sometimes a single event that raised their suspicion enough to bring it to the attention of the pediatrician. That event became part of a story that followed the child throughout early life. For example:

- A mother tells how she woke up before the alarm went off and checked the sleeping baby in the bassinet next to the bed. The alarm then rang loudly. It startled her but she couldn't help noticing that the baby did not respond.

- A father tells about the time his baby was asleep on the screened porch during a Fourth of July family gathering. He was carrying a tray full of barbequed meat from the yard to the kitchen. He walked through the porch and let the screen door slam shut. Looking at the sleeping baby as he walked by, he noticed that she did not stir in response to the sound.

These stories marked important milestones in the way these parents came to know their children in the context of hearing loss. They were recounted with pride and a sense of confidence in their ability to take care of a child with hearing loss. These parents felt that they played an important role in detection and diagnosis and that this was preferable to receiving devastating information from a stranger before taking the baby home from the hospital.

And everything that was said in Chapter 8 about being aware of sounds and bringing them to the child's attention applies to sounds associated with the activities of people in the house.

The Observation Principle

Rationale

The parent-child relationship is characterized by intimacy. Professionals who intervene in this relationship must tread carefully and with respect. Actions, statements, and suggestions should be based on knowledge and understanding of the child, the family, and their everyday interaction. Personality, capacity, and learning style differ from child to child, and parents have differences of experience, perception, knowledge, belief, culture, and interactive style. It takes time to see, appreciate, and understand these differences and to recognize where there may be a need and an opportunity for positive change. Counseling and coaching of parents, which we refer to as indirect intervention, should begin with observation rather than interrogation, advice, or instruction.

Implications

One implication is that observation should occur in the family's own environment and during activities of everyday living. Home visits provide a good setting for observation. Faced with the logistical problems associated with this approach, however, some programs have established model homes within their centers as an effective alternative.

As the child and family are interacting, the professional should watch and listen. He should make note of behaviors such as proximity, use of voice, facial expression, patterns of touch, the infant's emotional and social responsiveness, and her anticipation of, and responses to, sensory stimulation. Does the child show excitement and enthusiasm before being picked up by Mom? Does she enjoy being thrown in the air by Dad? Does she ask for repetition? How are requests conveyed? Does she initiate interaction? Do the adults acknowledge and respond to her efforts? Does she explore? Does she smile and/or vocalize when the hearing aids are turned on? Are her utterances and nonverbal signals differentiated on the basis of intent? How are conflicts resolved? Is there evidence of mutual enjoyment of between child and family ? Note also the parents' affect. Does it convey excitement, enthusiasm, and enjoyment to the child or does it convey fatigue, boredom, worry, or lack of interest? Are the parents behaving naturally and ignoring the fact that they are being observed or are they self-conscious, trying to impress, or avoid embarrassment?

Once the professional is confident in his conclusions about the child, the parents, their behaviors, and their relationships, he can comment on his observations, calling attention to the interactions that are positive in fostering the social relationship. It also may be appropriate to draw the parents' attention to specific interactions that have been observed, to discuss possible implications, and perhaps make suggestions about enhancement, modification, and alternatives. Note that we say "may be." Careful assessment of the parents' readiness for suggestions is also important. Remember, also, that the focus, in this chapter, is not on the use and maintenance of hearing assistance or on spoken language, but on the child's social-emotional development and the role played by parent-child attachment and interaction.

Note, finally, that the success of this aspect of the work depends on the developing relationship between parent and professional. As in all working relationships, issues of trust, respect, reciprocity, comfort, and enjoyment are important. Differences of personality, interactive style, beliefs, and culture between the professional and the parent can threaten this developing relationship if they are not recognized and addressed. We will have more to say about this issue in Chapter 12.

The Novelty Principle

Rationale

Routines make an environment more predictable for everyone but particularly for children with limited hearing and language.

Routines help children anticipate what comes next and partici-
pate in the activity more fully. Routines provide opportunities for
using predictable language in the form of scripts. The boundaries
imposed by routines allow children freedom to explore. The sense
of mastery and participation that comes from routines helps build
self-confidence and contributes to a positive self-image.

On the negative side, overly regimented environments and
repetitive activities can undermine the incentive for exploration,
learning, and creativity. Children also need the challenge of novelty. Mastery of new challenges helps build a sense of competence
and contributes to self-confidence and a positive self-image.

Implications

When interacting with the child, parents and professionals should
aim for a balance between the predictable and the new. This is not
always easy. Children differ in terms of their need for routine and
their tolerance for novelty. Moreover, the same child may be more
tolerant of novelty on some days than on others. This is another
example of the need for careful observation. Children will usually
provide behavioral cues when they are bored with the predictable
or overwhelmed by the new. Healthy social-emotional development is more likely when adults can interpret these cues and make
responsive, accommodating, adjustments in their behavior and
expectations.

The Limits Principle

Rationale

Adults limit children's behavior to keep them safe, to help them
learn to regulate themselves, and to create conditions that are
comfortable and culturally acceptable. Behavioral limits can be
enforced and managed effectively by adults when they are few in
number; when the limits and the reasons for them are understood

by the child; when there is agreement about them among the adults in authority; and when they are consistently reinforced. It can be difficult to believe during an emotional meltdown, but children are relieved when adults establish and enforce clear limits.

In toddlerhood, behavioral limits are usually focused on safety and social acceptability (NO running into the street, NO hitting, NO biting, NO taking someone else's things, and so on). These taboos are generally easy to convey by words, gestures, and pictures. Restrictions and rules should be paired with explanation of reasons and presentation of safer or more acceptable alternatives.

Parents might be more permissive with a deaf child than with a hearing sibling. They may feel that behavioral accountability is not reasonable for children with hearing loss because they may not understand the reason for a particular restriction. Or, they may feel badly about limiting behavior in a child who they feel already lives with limitations imposed by hearing status. Whatever the reason, unclear or intermittently reinforced limits can reduce access to the social world, and limit opportunities for social-emotional growth.

Implications

The primary implication is for parents and other adults involved in caregiving to discuss and agree on limits, consequences, and consistency of reinforcement. At the same time, they should be aware of the child's need for a sense of control and agree on areas within which the child gets to choose. For example, insisting on a specific time for bed may be a good thing. But the development of autonomy is supported by allowing the child freedom in choosing bedtime attire, a toy to take to bed, or deciding whether lights are left on or turned off.

Parents should not be dismayed when their child continually tests the limits. This is part of the developmental process. Children experiment to see if limits, and their enforcement, might vary with time, situation, place, identity of the adult, mood of the adult, presence of other people, and so on. Conflict is especially noticeable during toddlerhood. This is a time when the child has developed an understanding that other people have perceptions, desires, and emotional reactions, but he now has to deal with the discovery that they can be different from, and in conflict with, his own. The behaviors that lead parents to describe this phase as the "terrible twos" are a result of the child's experimentation with new-found abilities and her attempts to understand and resolve these conflicts.

In dealing with conflicts, it helps if parents can remain calm. The child's discovery that his actions produce parental stress is an invitation to explore and perfect this avenue for control. Remaining calm also creates an opportunity for parents to acknowledge and verbalize the child's desires and emotional reactions. It is good to acknowledge feelings while conflicts are in process, even though this slows things down. We realize the difficulty of staying calm and talking about what is happening. But extra time and a slower pace can allow both parties to assimilate and talk about the emotional reactions as they are happening and everyone can benefit from the experience.

Note that the ultimate goal for setting and reinforcing limits that go beyond simple issues of safety is that the child will self-regulate, especially in relation to behaviors that affect others. The resulting social competence will open the doors to more opportunities for interaction, social-cognitive development, and the formation of friendships. Do we need to say it again? This is another example of positive feedback; the more socially and emotionally competent the child, the greater the opportunity for further social emotional development.

The Acknowledgment Principle

Rationale

In the previous section, we referred to the need to acknowledge the child's emotional reaction to an imposed limit on behavior. The same principle applies to all emotional reactions. It is never appropriate to tell someone that they should not be experiencing a particular feeling, least of all a child who is just beginning to learn what emotions mean. The emotion is what it is. It has a

Who Chooses Bedtime?

Jimmy: (Vigorously pointing to the door). Uh! Uh! Uh!

Mother: (Nodding and frowning). You want to go outside to play with your new scooter. You want to go round and round the yard as fast as you can—like you did this afternoon. I know you want to go out to play with your scooter. But it's dark outside. I see the moon. Look. There's the moon. (Smiling) And it's time for your bath—and then a bedtime story.

Jimmy: (Hanging onto the door knob) Begins to cry.

Mother: (Nodding and frowning) You are angry that you cannot play outside. You are disappointed that you cannot ride your scooter one more time. (Picks up child but maintains facial contact) I know you are angry. (Nodding and showing pleasure) But it's time for your bath and then bed and a story. Tomorrow you will ride your scooter again. I wonder which book you will choose tonight?

Jimmy: (Still whimpering, reluctantly complies).

Note: (a) Mother confirmed that the message was received; (b) she acknowledged Jimmy's feelings; (c) one hopes she used appropriate gestures and facial expressions to compensate for the child's limited language skills, (d) she remained calm, and (e) the established bedtime was maintained.

If Mother had ignored the impending tantrum and roughly carried Jimmy off to bathe, this would have confirmed his low social status, lack of autonomy, and inability to communicate his wishes and feelings. Before their behavior is restricted, children at risk for communication breakdown need to know that authoritative adults understand what they want, what they are trying to convey, and how they feel.

purpose as a catalyst in eliciting behaviors that establish emotional equilibrium. The child has no immediate mechanism for changing emotion. The emotion, however, can be acknowledged and labeled, and its cause explored.

Other areas calling for acknowledgment are effort and accomplishment. Problem solving and skill mastery promote a sense of achievement and they inspire pride and confidence. Learning to do such things as walk, talk, read, complete jigsaws, open containers, and fasten buttons requires repetitive attempts and practice, and usually involves some failure before mastery. Overcoming initial failure is important in learning. Parents of children with hearing loss, however, may want to protect them from the experience of failure. The desire can reflect an effort to compensate for limitations imposed by the deafness or language delay. But if children have no experience of coping with and overcoming failure, they are deprived of an opportunity to develop a sense of competence in their ability to solve problems and master challenges.

Finally, children need to know that adults are interested in their communication efforts and are making an effort to interpret and understand them. The underlying message may not be obvious from the child's verbal or nonverbal efforts. A simple question, for example, can be a genuine request for explanation or an indication that the child wants to maintain interaction (as in the "Why?" game). Sometimes, it is an indirect expression of internal struggle. In the next chapter, we talk about the importance of distinguishing content from emotion when counseling parents but the same issue exists when interacting with children—perhaps even more so. Social-emotional development is promoted when adults listen carefully to children and to the messages and intent behind the words.

Implications

The first implication for parents is that they should not evaluate feelings expressed by their children. Emotional expression is not bad or good, nor should it be suppressed or denied. Instead, parents should identify and acknowledge overt emotional reactions—labeling and discussing feelings, and talking about their causes. Reacting in this way helps the child learn more about her emotional self. This recommendation applies as much to expression of positive emotions (e.g., happiness, excitement, anticipation) as it does to negative ones (e.g., anger, sadness, disappointment). In short, adults should talk to children about their feelings.

A Sick Grandma

"Grandma won't be able to visit today. She just telephoned to say she is sick. She is not coming. Oh, what a *sad* face! I know you are *disappointed*. Every week Grandma comes to visit and she always brings you something nice. You were *excited* that she was coming and now you are *disappointed*. I am *disappointed* too. And I'm *sad* because Grandma is sick. I bet Grandma is *upset* that she can't be here. I hope she gets better soon. Hey! Let's make a card for Grandma. We can draw something she *likes* and tell her we *want* her to get better. What will you draw? What do you think Grandma would *want* to see?"

Later: "You drew some pretty flowers. And you did a great job of writing your name. When Grandma gets this card she will probably feel very *happy*. I think you did something very nice for Grandma. Here! You can put the stamp on the envelope and we'll mail it to Grandma"

How many "feeling words" were used in this simple exchange?

A second implication is that adults should acknowledge and reinforce effort and accomplishment, again, adding appropriate language. If the child becomes obviously frustrated and discouraged by failure, by all means help out or simplify the task, but acknowledge the effort—and the emotion of frustration.

A third implication is the importance of listening to the child, especially for indications of feelings or internal conflicts. Make it clear to the child that she is being heard and that what she feels and conveys is important to the listener. We already talked about responding to overt emotional responses. Here, we are talking about suppressed, hidden, or camouflaged feelings.

Content or Feeling?

Five-year-old Colin is being readied for school and things are not going well. His irritation comes to a head when he objects to putting on his hearing aids. "Why do I have to wear hearing aids?" he says. This is probably not a question about etiology, integrity of the cochlea, or rules. Most likely the underlying question is, "Why am I different from other children?" It can be difficult and upsetting for a parent to hear the emotional message behind the question. If it is interpreted as a content question, the parent might respond, "You have to wear hearing aids so you can hear better" or "You have to wear hearing aids because your ears don't work well." If, however, it is interpreted as an emotional question, an appropriate response might be, "I think you don't want to go to school today. It must be hard being the only kid in your class with hearing aids. Sometimes being different stinks. I bet you get angry at your hearing aids?"

Although this may not solve the problem at hand, at least it lets the child know the parent is listening to more than words.

Finally, parents should be encouraged to express and talk about their own feelings. The child's progress in identifying, labeling, talking about, and managing her emotional life is furthered when parents understand their own emotional landscape and lead by example.

The Play Principle

Rationale

In Chapter 10, we pointed out that play is an ideal context for spoken language development. It is also an ideal context for social-emotional development. There is no single, universal definition of the word "play"; a quick Internet search turns up many. There are, however, several identifying characteristics. Play is usually voluntary and self-initiated. It is not imposed by circumstances or by persons in authority. Unlike work, play has no obvious ulterior motive or goal. Play is its own reward. Most of all, play is pleasurable and fun. There is a tendency to think of play as trivial, but observation and research have shown it to be important in all aspects of development. In infants, play is the primary context for sensorimotor, cognitive, social-emotional, communicative, and linguistic learning. With maturity, the importance of play diminishes but never to zero. Even in adults, play promotes personal growth and maintains social-emotional integrity. The contributions of play to development are not restricted to humans but can be observed in many other species, especially those that rely on social groups for survival.

This brings us to our present concern, which is the role of play as a context for early social-emotional development of the child with hearing loss. Early mastery of sensorimotor skills during solitary play leads to pride in accomplishment and increased self-confidence. Interactive play between parent and child reinforces attachment. As children mature, the beginnings of social interaction with other children are seen in parallel play, eventually leading to shared play. One aspect of shared play is that the activities are no longer entirely self-initiated. Reciprocity becomes essential. Leadership must be shared or alternated. The resulting relationships advance communicative and social competence and provide benefits to both participants.

Symbolic, imaginative, creative, and role play are particularly helpful for the child who is struggling to adapt to a world in which others hear and speak without difficulty. One benefit is that she can control play in ways that don't work in the larger world. She chooses the topic; she sets the pace; and she increases the opportunity for practice and mastery (Figure 11–1).

Another benefit of play is that children tend to maintain attention longer when they are having fun. When play involves two or more people, the pleasure is shared and both parties feel relaxed and calm as a result (Figure 11–2).

Figure 11–1. In solitary play, the child chooses the topic, sets the pace, and provides herself with opportunities for imagination, control, and mastery. (Photograph courtesy of Clarke Schools for Hearing and Speech.)

Play can be motivated by a need to resolve an internal emotional conflict (e.g., playing firemen because of a scary experience with fire). It can also be motivated by an emotionally and socially significant event in the child's life (e.g., caring for baby dolls after the arrival of a new baby). Sometimes, the child communicates, through play, emotional struggles that he or she is unable to express in other ways. Attentive parents and clinicians can interpret these struggles from play behaviors, and, perhaps, expand, explore, and encourage verbal expression.

There are some who feel that the child with hearing loss should spend time more productively with adults in "teaching" situations. As we stressed in Chapter 10, however, it is the child

Figure 11–2. Shared cooperative play has social-emotional benefits for both parties. (Photograph courtesy of Clarke Schools for Hearing and Speech.)

who does the learning. The adult's task is to provide experiences that promote learning. Play, whether it is solitary, shared, symbolic, imaginative, or social, offers the ideal context for learning. Play can also have a positive effect on emotional state and shared play can have a positive effect on social function. As we said before, play is the work of childhood. For the child at play, job satisfaction is guaranteed (Figure 11–3).

Implications

The first implication is that the toys and activities of infants and toddlers should provide maximum opportunity for learning, problem-solving, and mastery during solitary play. We already said this

Figure 11–3. For the child at play, job satisfaction is guaranteed. (Photograph courtesy of Clarke Schools for Hearing and Speech.)

in relation to sensorimotor, cognitive, and conceptual development. Here, we are thinking of the positive benefits of learning and mastery on the child's perception of himself as a competent person.

The second implication is that parents should be encouraged to spend a significant amount of time playing with their child. Some parents do this instinctively, naturally, and with ease. Some do not, regardless of the child's sensory status. And some are able to play with a hearing child but find that the hearing loss, their emotional reactions to it, and a conviction that they are supposed to be the child's "teachers," inhibit the motivation to play. It may be difficult for them to realize that loving, enjoying, playing with, and talking to their child are the primary factors in promoting full emotional and social development. One of us remembers the comment of a former colleague, Dr. Angela Broomfield, who said, after emerging from a frustrating parent guidance session, "I seem to spend most of my time trying to show parents how to play with their children."

Daily caregiving activities such as: dressing, bathing, and feeding, provide opportunities for playlike interaction. They can be fun — especially if the parents can approach them without urgency. Adding play makes these activities more in tune with the child's desire to spend time interacting with parents (remember the "Spoon game" and the "Why? game"). The benefits to emotional development can be considerable. There is no better demonstration to a child of his inherent worth than parents who show pleasure in spending time playing with him.

Like parents, clinicians have extrinsic goals when interacting with a child. But, even in a therapeutic situation, the more the child can experience the interaction as play, the greater the likelihood of success. This is particularly true of behavioral hearing tests. Beginning students of pediatric audiology quickly learn that, if a child does not want to play with them, all their training in diagnostic and testing techniques becomes irrelevant. They also learn about the need for reciprocity if they want the child to play, at least part of the time, according to their rules.

A third implication is the need for play groups, preschools, and other contexts in which the child can experience shared play. Varied opportunities for play with other children can speed and enhance social-emotional development. By the time a deaf child is 3 years old, she is likely to have had considerable contact with early intervention specialists, teachers of the deaf, audiologists, speech pathologists, and child-care providers. The resulting interactions and relationships may be positive and fruitful but they are relationships in which the child has limited control. In contrast, a

TV or No TV? That Is the Question

Television is inherently attractive to infants. The color, move-ment, and sound in cartoons can engage an infant's attention regardless of content or plot. For this reason, the TV can be a welcome baby minder for parents dealing with multiple demands. The ideal learning situation for a developing child, however, is one in which the child's actions produce results. Only in this way can he acquire sensorimotor, cognitive, perceptual, conceptual, and communicative skills and derive satisfaction from a sense of mastery and control. Television offers much in the way of sensory input but it does little in terms of interaction. Apart from turning it on and changing channels, there isn't much a child can do to influence what he sees or hears. There is little to explore, there are few problems to solve, and virtually nothing to promote thinking. Although a little TV can do no harm, it should not be used as a substitute for more productive play activities, especially those involving interaction with parents.

For the toddler, things are a little different. Educational programming for young children can be designed to promote thinking, vocabulary development, social awareness, and expo-sure to early skills of literacy and numeracy. But, at this age, educational TV is, at best, a supplement. It should not be used as a substitute for playing with real objects, real children, and real adults.

preschool placement provides peer relationships and yields a con-text for learning about parity, fairness, cooperation, social norms, and cultural values. By age 4, children are developing a personal identity that includes such aspects as gender, age, size, race, eth-nicity, activity level, talents, extroversion/introversion, and hearing status. They do this by interacting with a variety of children with whom they share similarities and differences. The message, here, is simple. Social development occurs best in environments that involve social interaction.

Only One Implant?

Charlie is a 4-year-old boy with binaural cochlear implants and limited experience with other deaf children. He visited a preschool that serves both hearing and deaf children. There, he met Christine, a 4-year-old girl with a single implant. After he left the classroom, the teacher told him that Christine was going to get a second implant. Charlie said (with a tone of excitement) "Then she will be just like me!" His parents had told him repeatedly that he was very special because he had two implants. But it can be hard to be unique when trying to develop a sense of belonging.

The Modeling Principle

Children learn about emotional expression and social behavior from the adults around them. Delays and deficits in spoken language may make it difficult for children to understand verbal expressions and interactions but feelings and attitudes can be conveyed nonverbally. Demonstrating love and affection through physical contact, facial expressions, intonation patterns, gestures, and smiles sends a clear message to children that they are valued and accepted. Showing pride and excitement in their achievements and spending time with them also demonstrates appreciation, value, and respect.

Life is full of conflict and contention. Adults are often uncomfortable with confrontation, or argument. Sometimes they try to shield children from this kind of experience. Witnessing conflict, however, helps children to recognize, in others, the feelings they experience themselves. If they also see resolution of conflict, this provides reassurance and reduces anxiety that might have been aroused by such things as raised voices, angry faces, and tense body postures.

Prosocial behaviors are good antidotes for the antisocial. Examples include behaviors resulting from empathy and altruism. We talked, earlier, of empathy as experiencing in one's self the emotions demonstrated by another. Empathy is more complicated than sympathy, which we see as recognition and acknowledgment of others' emotions without necessarily sharing them. Altruism may be defined as acting to the benefit of another without considering the benefit, risk, or loss to oneself. Empathy and altruism contribute to healthy social and emotional development and are often introduced to children through storytelling. But the best learning comes from seeing evidence of them in real life. This is especially true for the child whose spoken language competence is at an early stage of development.

Implications

There is only one implication: to encourage healthy social-emotional development in the child, adults should be good examples.

Some Things to Remember

1. Social-emotional function drives **communication** which, in turn, provides the context for further development of language, cognition, and social cognition.

2. **Sound and hearing** can reduce surprise and anxiety and increase predictability in the environment by keeping the infant in touch with people and events in the environment.

3. Before beginning indirect intervention the professional should **observe** child and family in order to understand their social-emotional status and interactive styles.

4. The child's experiences should strike a balance between the security of the **predictable** and challenge of the **novel**.

5. Children benefit from clear and consistently enforced **behavioral limits**.

6. Social-emotional development is furthered by **acknowledging** the child's feelings, efforts, and accomplishments.

7. **Play** is an effective context for social-emotional development.

8. Prosocial behaviors and attitudes are best learned by **example**.

To Learn More

- For further reading on social-emotional development we again recommend *Nurtureshock: New Thinking About Children* (Bronson & Merryman, 2009).

- Another excellent resource is *Happy Child, Happy Adult* (Hallowell, 2005).

- A very accessible text on this topic is *Social and Emotional Development* (Riley, San Juan, Klinkner, & Ramminger, 2007).

- Social-emotional development in the preschool environment is covered in *Caring Classrooms/ Intelligent Schools* (Cohen, 2001).

- The topic of play and its role in social-emotional development are explored well in *The Power of Play* (Elkind, 2007).

- The concept of play as the work of childhood provides the orientation of *A Child's Work: The Importance of Fantasy Play* (Paley, 2004).

- For more insights on play, read *Supporting Play, Birth Through Age Eight* (Sluss, 2005).

CHAPTER 12

Families

In previous chapters, we made many references to the primary role of the family, especially parents, as creators of the learning environment for the child with hearing loss. Not only do parents create the environment, they are an integral part of it. Interactions between child and parents provide the context for early social-emotional, linguistic, and communicative development. Even as the child grows and learns from clinicians and teachers, the family still provides the primary context for cognitive, intellectual, emotional, social, and cultural learning.

The relationship between parent and child develops around the innate drives and capacities of both. These drives and capacities are supplemented, on the parent's side, by explicit knowledge, beliefs, and aspirations resulting from life experience and cultural background. Under ideal circumstances, the learning process within the relationship is mutual, synchronous, harmonious, and elegant; like the running of a well-designed and well-oiled machine.

Unfortunately, when a child with hearing loss is born into a hearing family, a situation that applies to at least 9 of 10 children with hearing loss, a wrench is thrown into the works. There are three major consequences:

1. In addition to regular child-rearing responsibilities, the parents now must acquire a body of knowledge about hearing, hearing loss, and hearing devices; they must learn about the benefits and limitations of various approaches to intervention; and they need to enrich the child's learning environment, and

their interactive style, to compensate for the hearing loss and its developmental consequences.

2. Many of the instinctive behaviors of parents require appropriate responses from the child for their reinforcement and continuation. Failure of the child to respond as expected can result in an impoverished learning environment rather than an enhanced one.

3. At the same time, parents must deal with their emotional response to the diagnosis of hearing loss. The initial response can be intense and visceral and progress on other fronts may well be stalled until the parents have moved beyond this stage. They need time to adapt to their shock at the news, their loss of the child they had anticipated, and their sense of inadequacy in facing the looming challenges. The emotional response subsides but will never vanish entirely. It is likely to resurface every time the child transitions to a new stage of development. Each time, however, the parents' reaction becomes more manageable, especially when there is support from family, community, and professionals.

Support from professionals provides the focus of this chapter. Much of what we have discussed in previous chapters dealt with *direct* intervention, that is, interactions between parent and child or between professional and child. In this chapter, we deal with *indirect* intervention, that is, interaction between professional and parent. The distinction between direct and indirect intervention is illustrated in Figure 12–1.

Family Intervention

There are several goals of family intervention: (a) to provide support as parents work through their emotional reactions to the diagnosis of their child's hearing loss, (b) to help parents acquire the

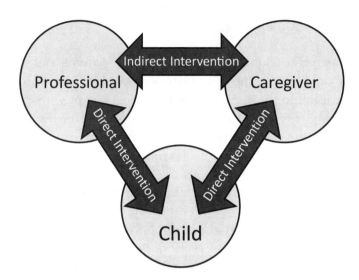

Figure 12–1. For the very young child with hearing loss, professional intervention in the developmental process is indirect. It occurs through interaction with caregivers. As the child grows, professionals may spend more time intervening directly with the child, but the importance of indirect intervention remains.

practical knowledge they will need as they deal with the child and the loss, (c) to help parents acquire practical skills needed for optimizing hearing capacity and hearing skill, (d) to help parents promote the child's cognitive and language development, and (e) to help parents promote their child's social-emotional development.

Pursuit of these goals can take several forms. Here, we identify five.

Adjustment Counseling

The professional interacts with the parents. Most of the time is spent in active listening. The goal is to speed and optimize the parents' adjustment process as they deal with their emotional reactions. We say more about active listening later.

Informational Counseling

Again, the professional interacts with the parents but now the focus is on helping them acquire knowledge. This knowledge will contribute to their evolving effectiveness as parents of a child with hearing loss. Part 1 of this text covers some of these instructional needs but parents can differ dramatically in terms of their prior knowledge, learning style, learning preferences, and learning capacity. The professional needs to have a variety of resources to which she can refer parents for more information, or for the same information presented in a different way.

Much can be gleaned about the informational learning needs of parents from careful observation. For parents who are reflective and articulate, direct questions may be helpful; for example: "How do you learn new things?" "What's the best way to help you learn about the work we do here?" "Would you like pamphlets and books?" "How about videotapes of our sessions to share with your family?" "How's your access to the Internet?" A particularly good learning opportunity for the professional lies in the form and content of questions asked by the parents. These questions are more likely to be frequent and revealing if the professional and the parents have developed a relationship of trust, honesty, and mutual respect.

One goal of instructional counseling is to help parents as they make decision. Parents of children with hearing loss are faced with many decisions related to management. Are they going to opt for cochlear implants? Will they introduce sign language? Should they consider a specialized preschool setting or the local public preschool program? Some decisions dramatically alter the course of the child's and family's development.

The viability of various options often depends on the degree and type of hearing loss, the nature and capacities of the child, available resources, and the values and beliefs that parents bring to child rearing. As parents make and execute their decisions, the professional provides support and information. It is not the professional's role to advocate for a specific decision based on his or her own beliefs or biases. The goal is to help the parents learn what they need to know to make informed decisions. If discussing mutually exclusive options, for example, it is important to point out not only the benefits of each but also the potential drawbacks, and to talk about what may be involved in maximizing the benefits and minimizing the drawbacks. The distinction between informational counseling and advocacy must be recognized.

For the audiologist, much of the information provided will be about the audiogram and the purpose, function, use, care, and management of hearing aids or cochlear implants.

Demonstration

The professional interacts with the child in a play/teaching situation while the parents observe. The process has several goals. First, it helps establish the professional/child relationship. Second, the professional learns more about the child through diagnostic teaching. Third, it provides an opportunity for the professional to talk about what she is doing, why she is doing it, how the child is responding, and what it means. In other words, it contributes to parent learning. Fourth, it provides the parents with a model of an interactive style which they may (or may not) wish to emulate. Finally, it can contribute to learning on the part of the child.

On this last point, however, we stress that, for the infant, the amount of time spent in professional-child interaction is a drop in the bucket compared with the time spent in parent-child interaction. The goal, here, is not to train the child but to learn about the child and help the parents create an enriched environment to promote her development. Once the child is in preschool, of course, the contribution of professional/child interaction to the child's development becomes much more significant.

For the audiologist, much of the demonstration will deal with the use, care, and management of hearing aids or cochlear implants.

Coaching

The parent interacts with the child in play or an activity of everyday living and the professional observes. The professional may then comment on his or her observations. The observations help the professional learn about the parents, the child, their interactions, and their relationship. The parents also have an opportunity to learn, as the professional points out things about the interactions, draws attention to things they did well, and possibly makes suggestions about things that could be done even better. Once again, a relationship of trust and honesty helps reduce the potential for parents feeling they are being judged and found wanting. The goal is to increase their confidence, not undermine it.

The audiologist has initial responsibility for coaching in the use, care, and management of hearing aids or cochlear implants, but other professionals must be able to address this need on a continuing basis.

Enhancing Perspective

One of the most helpful things for parent learning is the chance to discover that they are not alone and that the future is hopeful. To this end, the professional can arrange for parents to meet or interact with other parents who are at a later stage in the process of raising a child with hearing loss. He or she can also provide opportunities to observe older children who have developmental capacities similar to their child, and whose developmental outcomes are related to some of the decisions made by their parents at an earlier age. It also can be useful for parents to meet adults with prelingually acquired hearing loss who are raising a family, engaging in rewarding work, and generally experiencing a satisfying life. It is important, however, that the professional exercise care in the choice of encounters. At this vulnerable stage, the parents are not helped by interaction with individuals who believe their primary role to be one of advocacy or who desperately need to justify their own choices. Nor are they helped by seeing amazing spoken language skills in a child whose assisted hearing capacity is much greater than that of their own child.

The choice and balance among these various activities should be determined, not by some predetermined curriculum, but by the characteristics, needs, learning style, and developmental status of the child; the characteristics, needs, learning style, and progress of the parents; the specific role of the professional (audiologist, speech-language pathologist, auditory-verbal therapist, teacher of the deaf, early intervention specialist), and the quality of the evolving relationship the professional has with both child and parents.

Families are complicated and diverse. They are affected by cultural beliefs and values in the extended family and society at large. Early family relationships influence who we are and how we form relationships as adults. The professional who is providing ongoing counseling, instruction, and guidance to the hearing family of a deaf child must get to know the child in the context of the family. Only then can he or she influence the family's learning in the most effective and positive way. Accomplishing this goal is easier when some work is done in the family's home. Unlike the situation in the clinic or preschool, the professional has no control over the complexity of home life. Yet, that environment provides the best opportunity to learn about the child and the family, and it is the environment in which the child will do most of his learning.

Active Listening

The initial diagnosis of deafness can be devastating for hearing parents who have had little or no contact with hearing loss. As they deal with the unexpected news, they are in no position to absorb or remember anything that follows. Unfortunately, a common reaction to discomfort by the bearer of bad news is to talk (Figure 12–2). At best, this is unproductive. At worst, it alienates the parents, and the chance that they will remember anything is slim. It is appropriate, however, to validate feelings ("This must be very upsetting for you"), to offer to answer any questions the parents may have, and to schedule a follow-up meeting soon after the initial diagnosis. If parents do ask questions, it is important to distinguish emotion-driven questions from content-driven questions. For example, "Why is this happening to us?" is not a cue to launch into a lecture on recessive genes or the vicissitudes of life. It is appropriate, however, to provide simple, nontechnical materi-

Figure 12–2. There is a serious limit to what parents can absorb after just learning their baby has a hearing loss.

als that parents can take and peruse at their own pace. Providing them with your contact information conveys a willingness to accept telephone calls or E-mails if they need to talk before the next meeting. And it is appropriate to ask if it would be acceptable to contact them in a few days to find out how they are doing. If there is a team member who will be providing indirect intervention this can be a good time to provide contact information and schedule an initial meeting. What the parents need most at this stage is validation and acceptance of the feelings that are engulfing them, reassurance that they have a lifeline to knowledgeable, understanding, and supportive professionals, and a realization that, at this stage, the hearing loss has no effect on the child's needs.

More About Shock, Grieving, and Coping

When parents are first told that their child has a hearing loss they usually react with shock. This can be experienced as a sinking feeling in the stomach, increased heart rate, disturbances of breathing, and throbbing in the temples. The individual in this state has very limited ability to process information, to think rationally, or to consider options. Shock is an appropriate and protective reaction to perceived threat in many species. In the present case, the perceived threat is to the social and cultural bond between parent and child and to the parents' own lifestyle and identity. They are facing the loss of the "perfect child," the child in their own image, and the relationship that they had believed was in their future.

Once they overcome the initial shock, parents are better able to process information and to learn about implications and options. But they must still go through a process of grieving. Analogies have been drawn between parental reactions to a diagnosis of hearing loss and the grief reaction to the death of a loved one. This model may be helpful, but there is an important difference. Parents of children with hearing loss live with chronic grief, that ebbs and flows throughout childhood, and even beyond. As the child develops and matures, new challenges arise. Transitions to preschool, elementary school, high school, dating, college, work, marriage, and so on are all opportunities for questions and uncertainties to re-emerge. No two parents go through the processes of grieving in the same way, in the same sequence, at the same rate, or for the same length of time.

As parents cope with and adapt to the reality of their child's hearing loss, they become more knowledgeable, more effective, and more confident in their ability to meet her needs. Once again, however, parents differ in terms of the speed, effectiveness, and outcome of the adjustment process.

Even after parents have recovered from the initial shock and are coping with their emotional reactions, active listening is still one of the professional's most powerful tools for successful intervention. Listening not only helps parents work through their adjustment but it also helps the professional to get to know the parent and it helps establish trust. If, at this time, parents ask questions about content, it is appropriate to provide information. It can take insight and experience, however, to distinguish content-driven questions from emotion-driven questions. If a parent asks, "What can I do to keep Kevin from pulling out his hearing aids?" she is probably seeking practical suggestions. But if she says, "Why do hearing aid batteries cost so much?" she may be expressing frustration at the many complications the hearing loss has introduced into her life. Acknowledging the frustration is likely to be more fruitful than talking about the costs of manufacture and distribution. As they make progress in accepting the hearing loss as part of their child, and their own roles as parents of a child with hearing loss, the professional's ratio of listening to talking will decrease, but the need for active listening never goes away.

Professional Development

The child and the parents are not the only ones who need to learn. The professional should never stop learning about the field and about him or herself. Every child, every family, and every interaction provide an opportunity for learning, which can be of three kinds:

1. **Knowledge base.** First, there is the professional's own knowledge base dealing with such things as hearing, hearing loss, hearing devices, speech, language, child development, and so on. Part 1 of this text provides only a cursory introduction to these topics. Full mastery requires a lifetime of learning. The importance of continued study, and keeping up with new developments, cannot be stressed enough. It is accomplished through reading, thinking, interacting with other professionals, attending lectures, and attending conferences. Fortunately, recent

More About Active Listening

Active listeners do:

- show attention with body language, eye contact, and minimal verbal encouragers ("Hm, Hm," "go on," "tell me more").

- ask open-ended questions ("What kinds of things do you notice?").

- help the listener to stay on the topic ("What was it you were saying about the high chair?).

- paraphrase and clarify ("You seem to be saying you are bothered when people talk to her with exaggerated mouth movements").

- make adjustments based on observations of the speaker's reactions ("Perhaps we should deal with this in more depth at our next meeting").

- encourage expressions of feeling (How did that make you feel?").

- acknowledge and reflect feelings ("That must be very worrying").

Active listeners do not:

- retreat behind physical barriers such as a desk or table.

- interrogate with "Yes/No" and "Why" questions ("Does she wear the aid all day?" "Why do you let her do that?").

- give direction ("You must make her keep the hearing aid in").

- lecture or reprimand ("If you let her get away with that, she will never . . . ").

- interrupt parents when they are trying to express or explain something.

- deny feelings ("There's no reason to feel angry").

- claim impossible insights ("I know how you feel").

developments in technology and methods of distance learning have increased opportunities for professional development.

2. **Skill base.** The second kind of learning deals with the skills of working with parents. Here, the work itself is the primary learning laboratory. Every encounter with every family should be examined for what it may add to the accumulation of expertise. Both successes and failures provide feedback and contribute to learning. But failures and mistakes probably contribute the most. Figuring out what can be learned from them is more valuable than denial or self-recrimination.

3. **Self-knowledge.** The decision to intervene in family relationships requires an interesting mixture of arrogance and humility. It should not be undertaken without introspection and care. The ultimate goal is knowledge, competence, and empowerment on the part of the parents, evidence for which comes when they don't need the professional any more. If professionals find themselves enjoying and perpetuating the dependence of parents, it is time for a serious examination of motivation and emotional needs. The well-adjusted professional acknowledges the contribution of his or her own history, culture, and experience to the successes and limitations of work with parents and children. In some cases, a family experience has been a motivating factor in choosing this profession. But the advice to budding interventionists is, "Know yourself; recognize your professional strengths; acknowledge your limitations; and make sure your own emotional house in order before trying to intervene in someone else's." Good advice comes from the airline industry's instructions for an emergency: "Secure your own oxygen mask before helping someone else with theirs."

Acceptance

The grieving process is supposed to lead to acceptance. But parents may never fully accept their child's hearing loss. They can, however, accept their child along with the hearing loss. They can also

A Tale of Two Children

■ Mary's first child had a profound hearing loss. The family adjusted well to the situation and the child was well-integrated into the family and was progressing well in kindergarten when a second child with hearing loss was born. Among other things, Mary worried that the first child would feel badly if he saw that she was upset by the news of his baby sister's hearing status. With a little time and support, however, she worked through her feelings about parenting two children with hearing loss and dealing with more hearing aids, cochlear implants, early intervention services, and specialized schooling. This time the coping was speedier and Mary was soon fully available as a resource to herself and her family.

■ Joan had a daughter with profound hearing loss. She planned a first birthday party on the afternoon that the child was fit with hearing aids. Joan was consumed with worries about the aids and her daughter's future. For her, the party was a painful memory. When, after 5 years, Joan learned that her second child was deaf, she was initially devastated by the news. The boy was fit with hearing aids at a few weeks of age, however, and he and his family were immediately provided with early intervention services. A year later, the interventionist was visiting and, as she passed the dining room, she saw that it was filled with streamers, confetti, and slightly deflated balloons: the remains of the boy's first birthday party. Remembering the story of his older sister's disappointing celebration, the teacher asked about the party and how it compared to that of his sister. The mother said, "Oh, it was fun. It was just a birthday party."

In both examples, the parent had experienced serious emotional reaction to the second diagnosis of deafness but this reaction was different from the first in kind, severity, and speed of adjustment.

accept their role as parents of a child with hearing loss. And they can build confidence in their ability to fulfill that role. It takes time for parents to reach this stage. In the meantime, they are making good progress if they feel free to love, enjoy, and play with their child.

Evidence of the long life of the grieving process sometimes appears when parents have a second child with the same impairment. They may well experience some of the reactions they had to the news of the hearing loss of the first child, even when that child is growing and developing well. This reaction can surprise family members or professionals who have witnessed how well the family has appeared to accept the hearing loss. Parents of second-born children with hearing loss may be confident about their abilities to raise their new baby, but they also know that their life will be complicated with more hearing devices, more appointments, more professional relationships, and more special attention to language and education. Fortunately, the emotional reactions are likely to be less severe the second time around and adjustment is likely to be speedier. There is some benefit in having gone through this before.

In Summary

This chapter dealt with interactions between professional and parents. The goals of these interactions are to help parents work through their adjustment to the diagnosis of hearing loss, to provide them with the knowledge, skills, and emotional balance they will need to become effective parents of a child with hearing loss, and to help them create an environment and experiences for the child that will promote cognitive, linguistic, and social-emotional development. The topics discussed included:

- the roles of adjustment counseling, instructional counseling, demonstration, coaching, and perspective enhancement as tools to promote parent learning,

■ the futility of providing information while parents are in a state of shock after learning that their child has a hearing loss,

■ the importance of active listening when parents need to talk about emotions and concerns,

■ the need for professionals to develop good observational skills as a way of learning about the child and the parents,

■ the importance of continued learning and self-examination on the part of the professional, and

■ the elusive goal of parental acceptance of the hearing loss.

To Learn More

■ Dr. David Luterman has built a prodigious career around the topic of family intervention. He summarized what he has learned about this work in a paper entitled, "Ruminations of an Old Man: A Fifty-Year Perspective on Clinical Practice," which appeared in a text edited by Robert Fourie (Luterman, 2010). We strongly recommend reading it.

■ We also recommend Luterman's book *Counseling Persons with Communication Disorders, and their Families* (Luterman, 2008).

■ Another good resource is a multiauthored text edited by Luterman: *Children with Hearing Loss: A Family Guide* (Luterman, 2006)

■ The issues of grief and coping are addressed well in an article entitled "Families and Children with Hearing Loss: Grief and Coping" by Kurtzer-White and Luterman (2003).

■ Excellent insights on this topic are also found in *Counseling Children with Hearing Impairment and Their Families* by Kristina English (2002).

- A wonderful parent perspective is provided in the previously quoted book *If a Tree Falls: A Family's Quest to Hear and Be Heard* by Jennifer Rosner (2010). This memoir reveals the impact that two daughters' hearing losses had on a mother's reflections on herself, her family, and her heritage, both cultural and genetic.

- A guide for parents in the early stages of making decisions that follow a diagnosis of hearing loss in their child is provided in the third edition of *Choices in Deafness* by Susan Schwartz (2007). This text includes family case studies.

APPENDIX A

Laws

In 1975, the federal government passed the Education of All Handicapped Children act. This act specified the responsibilities of States and Local Education Authorities in relation to children with disabilities affecting their education. Since then, the law has been amended and renamed several times. At the time of writing, the most recent version dates to 2004, with detailed regulations being published in 2006. It is now the Individual with Disabilities Education Improvement Act (IDEA).

Part B of IDEA covers children aged 3 to 21 years. Three key requirements are:

1. Free Appropriate Public Education (FAPE). The meaning of "Free" and "Public" is clear. The meaning of "Appropriate," however, has been a source of debate.

2. The Least Restrictive Environment (LRE). This expression can also be a source of debate. The intent is that education with non-disabled children should be the first choice but it is not an absolute requirement.

3. Individualized Educational Plan (IEP). The intent, here, is that the program will be based on the capacities and needs of the child and will not be dictated by what is currently available, or by generic needs associated with the disability in question. An important aspect of the IEP is the involvements of parents in drawing it up and approving it.

An early amendment was the inclusion of children aged birth to 3 years. This is covered in Part C of the current law. For infants and toddlers, the IEP is replaced by an Individualized Family Service Plan (IFSP). The concepts of "Free," "Appropriate," and "Public" still apply. The issue of Least Restrictive Environment is not relevant at this age, but the law suggests that work with children 0 to 3 years of age be carried out in a "natural environment" that is open to interpretation. "Natural environment" can be interpreted as "the home," which may or may not be the best environment for the early intervention work to take place, depending on the needs of the family and the early intervention resources available.

This law is clearly relevant to the current text. Our focus, however, has been on development in general rather than education in particular. Education clearly plays a role in human development, but cannot be considered to the exclusion of social-emotional function. For example, the least restrictive environment educationally may well by highly restrictive socially and emotionally. Note, also, that this text begins with the assumption that the child's parents are hearing and that spoken language has been established as a goal. No such assumptions are included in IDEA.

An excellent source of information on this topic is the National Dissemination Center for Children with Disabilities. They may be found online at http://nichcy.org/laws/idea . Information about interpretation of special education laws, regulations, and the IDEA can be found at http://www.wrightslaw.com/idea/art.htm .

APPENDIX B

SPLograms

In this text, we have adopted the practice of illustrating sound spectra and hearing thresholds on the audiogram form, where: the zero line represents the weakest sound that a typical person with normal hearing can detect at each frequency; threshold levels are expressed in dB HL (for Hearing Level); and increasing thresholds are represented by increasing distance *below* the zero line. This convention was adopted in the early days of audiometry with the idea that poorer (that is, higher) thresholds should be lower on the chart.

When measuring sound, however, especially sound entering and leaving a hearing aid, a different convention is usually used. The zero line represents sounds with a precise size of pressure fluctuations, independent of frequency; sound levels are then expressed in dB SPL (for Sound Pressure Level); and increasing levels are represented by increasing distance *above* the zero line.

When comparing hearing thresholds with speech spectra or hearing aid outputs on the same chart, one or the other must be modified so that both use the same zero level and both show increasing sound level in the same direction. Here we chose to change sound and hearing aid data to make them match the threshold data—this being the representation that most educators and interventionists are likely to be familiar with.

When comparing speech spectra with hearing thresholds, however, current practice is to express the thresholds in dB SPL and show them on the same chart that is used for sound measurement and hearing aid evaluation. An audiogram shown in this way is often referred to as an SPLogram. Modern hearing aid test systems actually show the spectrum of an amplified speech spectrum in relation to the SPLogram (entered by the audiologist). In Figure B–1, we show how Simon's audiogram and audibility for unamplified speech (Figure 6–4) would appear when represented in this way. Changing from one illustration to the other has no effect on the information conveyed or the conclusions drawn.

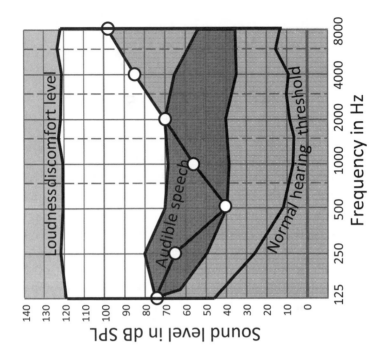

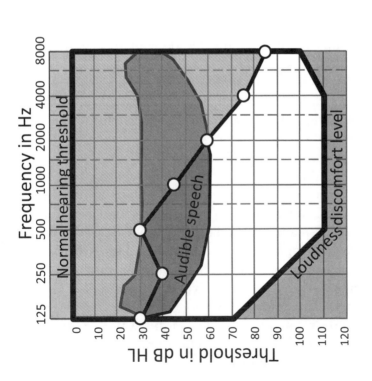

Figure B-1. The speech spectrum in relation to threshold shown on an audiogram form (*left panel*) and on an SPLogram form (*right panel*).

APPENDIX C

FM Amplification and Infants

Parent (P): I've been hearing about FM hearing aids. What are they?

Audiologist (A): An FM system uses a mobile microphone to pick up sounds and send them to a tiny radio receiver connected to a hearing aid.

P: Does it give higher fidelity because it is FM?

A: No. FM just stands for frequency modulation, which refers to the way the sound is carried from the microphone to the hearing aid. What makes the sound quality better is the fact that the microphone can be close to an important source of sound, such as your mouth.

P: So FM is not a different *kind* of hearing aid.

A: Correct. It is an *accessory* to a hearing aid.

P: Jennifer has the latest digital hearing aids. Why would she need an accessory?

A: Most of the time she doesn't. When she is already close to the source of the sounds that she needs to hear, there is no need for an extra microphone. But sometimes, important sounds are produced at a distance and need to travel through the air to reach her ears. Sounds get weaker as they travel, and by the time they reach her, they may be too weak to be heard properly. One of the beauties of a wireless microphone is that it picks up sounds at their source and sends them directly to the hearing aid without any loss of strength.

P: But I was told that Jennifer's hearing aid uses compression to increase the level of weak sounds from far away. Doesn't that take care of things?

A: Up to a point, yes. If you are out of doors, and it is very quiet, the compression circuits in the hearing aid may well be able to adapt by increasing the level of weak sounds. But there is usually some background noise (e.g., leaves rustling, wind blowing, traffic noise, etc.). As the sound travels and becomes weaker, it sinks into the noise and, by the time it reaches Jennifer's ear, the important sound and the noise are mixed together. The hearing aid has no way to separate them.

P: Aha! I was told that Jennifer's hearing aid has noise-suppression or noise reduction or something like that.

A: Unfortunately, a hearing aid isn't smart enough to know what kinds of sound Jennifer needs to hear and what should be classified as noise. The best a noise management program can do is to reduce the overall level of sound when it decides the mixture is mostly noise. If you leave the radio on during a news report while you are talking to Jennifer, the hearing aid may think that the voice from the radio is what Jennifer is listening to, rather than background noise. And sometimes it will think that something is noise when it is part of an important and meaningful sound she needs to hear clearly.

P So there is nothing to be done about noise?

A: Not exactly. The trick is to prevent noise from getting into the aid in the first place. The most effective way is to use a wireless microphone. This assumes, however, that the microphone is close to the source of the sounds that you want Jennifer to hear. This is usually your mouth, but it could be a newly hatched chicken.

P: Are you telling me that I should be using an FM system all the time?

A: Absolutely not. It all depends on the situation.

P: Give me an example.

A: Suppose Jennifer is in her playpen and you are on the other side of the room. If you have her attention, you could talk to her using the wireless microphone, knowing that she hears your voice as well as if you were right next to her. You might also want to get her attention by calling her name. Another example might be when you are driving the car and her baby seat is in the back. With the wireless microphone, you could talk to her, or sing to her, knowing that your voice at the microphone is louder than the car engine and traffic noise. And if she is in bed but not yet asleep, you could even talk or sing to her from another room.

P: It still sounds as though I should just use an FM microphone all the time.

A: Not a good idea. If you are already close to her, there is no need for the extra microphone. And there are times when it is more important for Jennifer to be hearing things going on around her. If she is playing with blocks, she should be hearing the sounds they make when they touch. If she is babbling or singing she should hear the sound of her own voice. She can't do this if you are engaged in a noisy activity, or talking to a friend, and wearing an active FM microphone. The sounds from your microphone could blot out the sounds that are important for her to hear. Remember, too, that a wireless microphone is like a wandering ear over which the child has no control. Having it turned on all the time would make it more difficult for Jennifer to figure out what is making sound and where it is coming from. Indiscriminate use of a wireless microphone is not good. The time when a wireless microphone can be valuable is when you want Jennifer to hear your speech and you are at some distance from her in noisy surroundings. Otherwise, she needs to be hearing the things around her—especially the sounds she makes herself. By all means purchase an FM system, but think carefully about what it is for, when it might be useful, and when it might create more problems than it solves.

APPENDIX D

Formal Tests

Possible reasons for administering formal tests include:

1. To establish the need for hearing assistance.

2. To determine the best option for hearing assistance.

3. To prescribe the characteristics of hearing assistance.

4. To measure the outcome of hearing assistance.

5. To plan other aspects of intervention—hearing skill, cognition, language, social emotional function.

6. To assess the outcome of these aspects of intervention and plan changes if necessary.

7. To add to a database for assessing program effectiveness.

In Chapter 6, we discussed tests of hearing threshold. These can be electrophysiologic, using the Auditory Brainstem Response (ABR), or they can be behavioral. In the latter category, the Ling test is useful for confirming audibility of key speech sounds. The presence of responses to a set of five or six sounds, spoken at levels typical of conversational speech, is sufficient to confirm audibility.

Hearing capacity, however, depends not only on threshold but also on resolution—the ability to detect significant differences among sound patterns. At the time of writing, there are no good electrophysiologic tests of resolution but research is underway that involves brain wave responses to change in an ongoing sound. Conditioned head turns in response to change in a stream of repeated syllables can provide useful information in children as young as 6 to 18 months. After around 3 years of age, children are ready for test involving imitation. Imitation of the sounds in the Ling test provides confirmation of the ability to differentiate them. More detailed information can be obtained from the imitation of nonsense syllables designed to reveal the detection of finer phonetic contrasts (Boothroyd, Eisenberg, & Martinez, 2010).

Several tests have been developed to assess emerging hearing skill. A popular test is the Meaningful Auditory Integration Scale (MAIS) by Robbins, Renshaw, and Berry (1991). A version for infants and toddlers (IT-MAIS) is intended for children between 6 and 36 months of age. It involves parent responses to 10 questions describing various activities that involve hearing. A copy is available on line at http://shop.advancedbionics.com/UserFiles/File/IT-MAS_20brochure_20_2.pdf * .

Another useful test is the Screening Instrument for Targeting Educational Risk (SIFTER), which also comes in a preschool version. A nice feature of this test is that it goes beyond issues of hearing capacity and skill and asks questions related to social-emotional function. Copies of this test can be obtained from The Educational Audiology Association at http://www.edaud.org/storelistitem.cfm?itemnumber=6 . The manual can be downloaded at http://www.kandersonaudconsulting.com .

Many other tests have been developed to assess hearing capacity, hearing skill, and the integration of hearing into development. Interested readers will find useful summaries in:

- *Incorporating Functional Auditory Measures into Pediatric Practice*, from the Oticon hearing aid company: http://www.oticonusa.com/eprise/main/SiteGen/Uploads/Public/Downloads_Oticon/Pediatrics/Inc_Functional_Measures_Guide.pdf

- A 1999 paper on *Hearing Aid Outcome Measures for Children* by Pat Stelmachowicz.

- Chapter 15, entitled, "Special Hearing Aid Issues for Children," in Harvey Dillon's 2001 text, *Hearing Aids.*

---

*Some of the Internet addresses included here are lengthy, and a single error in entering them will lead to frustration. Moreover, Internet sites are not guaranteed to remain unchanged over time. Readers are encouraged to do their own Internet searches for information on these tests.

One way to assess language development is through emerging vocabulary by picture identification. The Peabody Picture Vocabulary Test (PPVT) by Dunn and Dunn (2007), currently in its 4th edition, is widely used for this purpose. It has been standardized down to around 30 months of age. For a thorough description, see http://www.associatedcontent.com/article/2279045/the_peabody _picture_vocabulary_test.html?cat=15

A more comprehensive assessment of infant development is provided by the *Bayley Scales of Infant Development* (2005), currently in its 3rd edition. These scales provide measures of cognitive/linguistic, motor, and behavioral function. Their primary purpose is to identify infants at risk for developmental delay. Only persons who have received the appropriate training are authorized to use these scales. More information is available at: http://www .answers.com/topic/bayley-scales-of-infant-development .

Another comprehensive developmental assessment of children birth to age 6 is the Transdisciplinary Play-Based Assessment. The child plays in a natural situation with the parent while professionals observe and use developmental guidelines to evaluate areas of sensorimotor, cognitive, social-emotional, and communication and language development in the child. The instrument can be used for both assessment and to talk with the parents about play-based intervention. Developed by Toni Linder, it is available through Brookes Publishing: http://www.brookespublishing.com/store/ books/linder-tpbai2/index.htm .

These suggestions are offered as a starting point for readers interested in the issue of assessment. The limitations of formal testing, however, should be kept in mind. Children and their families are complicated entities. They cannot be pinned down by a series of numbers. True assessment is often informal and comes from professionals with a deep understanding of child development and family dynamics, supported by a good grounding in speech, hearing, and language.

References

Anderson, K. L. (1996). *Screening Instrument for Targeting Educational Risk (SIFTER)*. Preschool and school-age materials and manuals downloadable from kandersonconsulting.com .

Bailey Scales of Infant and Toddler Development (3rd ed.). (2005). San Antonio, TX: Pearson.

Berk, L. (2008). *Child development* (8th ed.). Boston, MA: Pearson/Allyn & Bacon.

Bodrova, E., & Leong, D. (2003). *Tools of the mind* (2nd ed.). Upper Saddle River, NJ: Pearson-Merrill/Prentice-Hall.

Boothroyd, A. (2008). The acoustic speech signal. In J. R. Madel & C. Flexer (Eds.), *Pediatric audiology* (pp. 159–167). New York, NY: Thieme.

Boothroyd, A., Eisenberg, L., & Martinez, A. (2010). An imitative test of speech-pattern contrast perception (OlimSpac): Developmental effects in normally hearing children. *Journal of Speech, Language, Hearing Research, 53,* 531–542.

Bronson, P., & Merryman, A. (2009). *Nurtureshock: New thinking about children.* New York, NY: Hachette Book Group.

Caldwell, L. (2003). *The Reggio approach: Bringing learning to life.* New York, NY: Teachers College Press.

Cohen, J. (Ed.). (2001). *Caring classrooms/intelligent schools: The social emotional education of young children.* New York: NY, Teachers College Press.

Cole, E., & Flexer, C. (2011). *Children with hearing loss: Developing, listening, and talking.* San Diego, CA: Plural Publishing.

Crandell, C. C., Smaldino, J. J., & Flexer, C. (2005). *Sound field amplification: Applications to speech perception and classroom acoustics.* Clifton Park, NY: Thomson Delmar Learning.

Davies, D. (2011). *Child development: A practitioner's guide* (3rd ed.). New York, NY: Guilford Press.

deVilliers, J., & deVilliers, P. (1978). *Language acquisition.* Cambridge, MA: Harvard University Press.

Dillon, H. (2001). *Hearing aids.* New York, NY: Thieme.

Dunn, L. M., & Dunn, D. M. (2007). *Peabody Picture Vocabulary Test, Fourth Edition (PPVT-4) manual.* Bloomington, MN: NCS Pearson.

Early Hearing Detection and Intervention (EHDI) Act of 2000. The original 2000 bill can be seen at: http://thomas.loc.gov/cgi-bin/query/z?c106: H.R.1193

Eisenberg, L. S. (Ed.). (2009). *Clinical management of children with cochlear implants.* San Diego, CA: Plural Publishing.

Elkind, D. (2007). *The power of play.* Philadelphia, PA: DaCapo Press.

English, K. M. (2002). *Counseling children with hearing impairment and their families.* Boston, MA: Allyn & Bacon.

French, N. R., & Steinberg, J. C. (1947). Factors governing the intelligibility of speech sounds. *Journal of the Acoustical Society of America, 19,* 90–119.

Furth, H. (1970). *Piaget for teachers.* Englewood Cliffs, NY: Prentice-Hall.

Gelfand, S. (2004). *Hearing: An introduction to psychological and physiological acoustics* (4th ed.). New York, NY: Marcel Dekker.

Gopnik, A., Meltzoff, A., & Kuhl, P. (1999). *The scientist in the crib.* New York, NY: William Morrow & Company.

Gutek, G. (Ed.). (2004). *The Montessori method.* Lanham, MD: Rowman & Littlefield.

Hallowell, E. (2005). *Happy child, happy adult: The childhood roots of adult happiness—a five-step plan.* UK: Vermilion Press.

Hirsh-Pasek, K., & Golinkoff, R. (2003.) *Einstein never used flash cards.* New York, NY: Rodale.

Hulit, L., Howard, M., & Fahey, K. (2006) *Born to talk: An introduction to speech and language development* (5th ed.). Upper Saddle River, NJ: Pearson Higher Education.

Joint Committee on Infant Hearing. (2007). Year 2007 position statement of the Joint Committee on Infant Hearing: Principles and guidelines for early hearing detection and intervention programs. *Pediatrics, 120,* 898–921. Summarized at http://www.asha.org/aud/articles/EHDI.htm

Kurtzer-White, E., & Luterman, D. (2003). Families and children with hearing loss: Grief and coping. *Mental Retardation and Developmental Disabilities Research Reviews, 9*(4), 232–235.

Killion, M. C., & Mueller, H. G. (2010). Twenty years later: A new count-the-dots method. *Hearing Journal, 63*(1), 10–17.

Lillard, P. (1997). *Montessori in the classroom: A teacher's account of how children really learn.* New York, NY: Schocken Books.

Linder, T. W. (2008). *Transdisciplinary Play-Based Assessment (TPBA2)* (2nd ed.). Baltimore, MD: Paul H Brookes.

Luterman, D. (2006). *Children with hearing loss: A family guide.* Sedona, AZ: Auricle Ink.

Luterman, D. (2008). *Counseling persons with communication disorders, and their families* (5th ed.). Boston, MA: Little Brown.

Luterman, D. (2010). Ruminations of an old man: A fifty-year perspective on clinical practice. In R. J. Fourie (Ed.), *Therapeutic processes for com-*

munication disorders: A guide for clinicians and students. New York, NY: Psychology Press.

Madell, J., & Flexer, C. (Eds). (2008). *Pediatric audiology.* New York, NY: Thieme.

Moeller, M. P. (2000). Early intervention and language development in children who are deaf and hard of hearing. *Pediatrics, 106,* e43. Accessible at http://pediatrics.aappublications.org/content/106/3/e43.full.pdf

Moeller, M. P., Donaghy, K. F., Beauchaine, K. L., Lewis, D. E., & Stelmachowicz, P. G. (1996). Longitudinal study of FM system use in non-academic settings: Effects on language development. *Ear and Hearing, 17,* 28–41.

Mueller, H. G., & Killion, M. C. (1990). An easy method for calculating the articulation index. *Hearing Journal, 9,* 14–17.

Northern, J., & Downs, M. (2002). *Hearing in children* (5th ed.). Baltimore, MD: Lippincott Williams & Wilkins.

Paley, V. (2004). *A child's work: The importance of fantasy play.* Cambridge: MA, Harvard University Press.

Pickett, J. M. (1999). *The acoustics of speech communication.* Needham Heights, MA: Allyn & Bacon.

Rehm, H. L., & Madore, R. (2008). Genetics of hearing loss. In J. Madell & C. Flexer (Eds.), *Pediatric audiology* (pp. 13–24). New York, NY: Thieme.

Riley, D., San Juan, R. R., Klinkner, J., & Ramminger, A. (2007). *Social and emotional development: Connecting science and practice in early childhood settings.* St. Paul, MN: Redleaf Press.

Robinson, A. M., Renshaw, J. J., & Berry, (1991). Evaluating meaningful auditory integration in profoundly hearing impaired children. *American Journal of Otology, 12*(Suppl.), 144–150.

Rosner, J. (2010). *If a tree falls: A family's quest to hear and be heard.* New York, NY: Feminist Press.

Roush, P. A. (2005). Hearing aid fitting in infants: Practical considerations and challenges. In R. C. Seewald & J. M. Bamford (Eds.), *A sound foundation through early amplification* (pp. 105–114). Basel, Switzerland: Phonak AG.

Roush, P. A. & Seewald, R. C. (2009) Acoustic amplification for infants: Selection, fitting, and management. In L. S. Eisenberg (Ed.), *Clinical management of children with cochlear implants* (pp. 35–58). San Diego, CA: Plural Publishing.

Schwartz, S. (2007a). *Choices in deafness* (3rd ed.). Bethesda, MD: Woodbine House.

Schwartz, S. (2007b). *The new language of toys: A guide for parents and teachers.* Baltimore, MD: Woodbine House.

Seewald, R., & Tharpe, A. M. (2010). *Comprehensive handbook of pediatric audiology.* San Diego, CA: Plural Publishing.

Sluss, D. (2005). *Supporting play: Birth through age eight.* Clifton Park, NY: Thompson Delmar Learning.

Speaks, S. E. (1999). *Introduction to sound: Acoustics for the hearing and speech sciences* (3rd ed). San Diego, CA: Singular Publishing Group.

Spivak, L., Sokol, H., Auerbach, C., & Gershkovich, S. (2009). Newborn hearing screening follow-up: Factors affecting hearing aid fitting by 6 months of age. *American Journal of Audiology, 17,* 24–33.

Stach, B. A., & Ramachandran, V. S. (2008). Hearing disorders in children. In J. Madell & C. Flexer (Eds.), *Pediatric audiology* (pp. 3–12). New York, NY: Thieme.

Stelmachowicz, P. G. (1999). Hearing aid outcome measures for children. *Journal of the American Academy of Audiology, 10,* 14–25.

Taylor, B., & Mueller, G. (2011). *Understanding hearing aids.* San Diego, CA: Plural Publishing.

The American National Standards Institute. (1969). *Methods for calculating Articulation Index.* S3.5,1969. Washington, DC: Author.

The American National Standards Institute. (1997*). Methods for the calculation of the Speech Intelligibility Index.* S3.5,1997. Washington, DC: Author.

Waldman, D., & Roush, J. (2009). *Your child's hearing loss: A guide for parents.* San Diego, CA: Plural Publishing.

Yoshinaga-Itano, C., Sedey, A. L., Coulter, D. K., & Mehl, A. L. (1988). Language of early-and later-identified children with hearing loss. *Pediatrics, 105,* 1161–1171.

Index